Wood n' Things

A Sole Proprietorship Merchandise Business

Linda Herrington, M.B.A., C.P.A.
Professor of Accounting
Community College of Allegheny County
Pittsburgh, Pennsylvania

John Ellis Price, Ph.D., C.P.A.
Professor and Chair
Department of Accounting
College of Business Administration
University of North Texas
Denton, Texas

M. David Haddock, Jr., Ed.D., C.P.A.
Professor of Accounting
Chattanooga State Technical Community College
Chattanooga, Tennessee

Horace R. Brock, Ph.D., C.P.A.
Distinguished Professor of Accounting Emeritus
College of Business Administration
University of North Texas
Denton, Texas

Glencoe
McGraw-Hill

New York, New York   Columbus, Ohio   Woodland Hills, California   Peoria, Illinois

CONTENTS

Cover: Michael Rohani
Wood n'Things Practice Set to accompany Price, Haddock, and Brock's *College Accounting, Ninth Edition.*

Send all inquiries to:
Glencoe/McGraw-Hill
936 Eastwind Drive
Westerville, OH 43081

ISBN: 0-02-804621-8

Printed in the United States of America.

1 2 3 4 5 6 7 8 9 10   073   03 02 01 00 99 98

INTRODUCTION TO THE BUSINESS

BACKGROUND

Wood n' Things is a retailer of contemporary wooden furniture and household accessories. The business is a sole proprietorship owned by Amy Glenn, who started it five years ago after a successful career as an executive at a local department store. The firm occupies a distinctive modern building, which complements its line of furnishings for today's houses and apartments.

LOCATION

Wood n' Things is located on Walnut Street, a small shopping district in the Shadyside section of Pittsburgh, Pennsylvania. Shadyside is a popular residential area. Three colleges are within walking distance, and the area is only seven minutes, via an express bus route, from the Golden Triangle, Pittsburgh's business district.

Walnut Street has many small boutiques that sell a wide range of items including high-fashion clothing, sportswear, toys, original works of art, antiques, and home furnishings. This variety makes Walnut Street a popular place to shop, attracting both local residents and residents of other areas of Pittsburgh. On Saturdays, in particular, the street is crowded with people who come to shop, browse, and eat at local restaurants.

Amy Glenn, the owner of Wood n' Things, is actively involved in promoting Shadyside as a unique place to shop and live. She has been president of the Shadyside Chamber of Commerce and organized the Shadyside Art Festival, which is held each August on Walnut Street.

FACILITIES AND LAYOUT

Wood n' Things sells its merchandise in a three-story brick building that it owns. This building is modern in design and features large windows facing the street for displaying merchandise. A unique feature is an open area alongside the entrance, which extends to the top of the building. This area is enclosed by a railing and is fronted by a two-story glass window, allowing people passing on the street and those entering the building to view merchandise on all levels of the store. This distinctive architecture draws attention and attracts customers to the store.

The interior of the building contains furniture groupings showcasing Wood n' Things furniture and accessories. Shelving, wall units, and desks are featured on the lower level with tables and chairs on the second floor and accessories such as lamps, table decorations, and gift items on the first floor. Part of the lower level is occupied by the stockroom and an administrative office is located at the rear of the first floor. A counter with a cash register and wrapping materials is located in front of the office. This arrangement allows the cashier access to the office files and keeps the cash register in clear view of the office staff.

On the street behind the building is a large municipal parking garage that provides parking space for people who want to visit Wood n' Things and the other stores on Walnut Street.

Wood n' Things operates a delivery van so that it can provide delivery service to its customers. The van is kept in a nearby garage, where the firm rents space.

PERSONNEL

Wood n' Things is managed by Amy Glenn, the owner, and has a staff of nine full-time employees. This includes the position of accountant, for which you have just been hired.

Name	Title	Duties
Amy Glenn	Owner and Manager	Manages store operations and supervises the entire staff. Authorizes all orders for new merchandise, and makes pricing decisions when merchandise arrives. Verifies all invoices prior to payment, and signs all checks. Responsible for staff training. Handles customer service problems and problems with suppliers. Does selling work during busy periods.
David Watson	Sales Supervisor and Assistant Manager	Supervises other salespersons and does some selling. Serves as assistant manager when Amy Glenn is away from the store.
Lisa Cohen	Interior Design Consultant	Responsible for selecting new stock and determining the overall style of the store's merchandise. Provides decorating assistance for customers.
Sally Nardozzi	Salesperson	Responsible for sales on the first floor. Maintains first floor stock.
Thomas Stevenson	Salesperson	Responsible for sales on the lower level. Maintains lower level stock.
James Demeter	Salesperson	Responsible for sales on the second floor. Maintains second floor stock.
Mike Willingham	Stockroom Supervisor	Manages the stockroom. Inspects new merchandise, and prepares receiving reports. Arranges for the transfer of merchandise to sales areas and for deliveries to customers. Keeps stockroom records. Responsible for attaching price tags to new merchandise. Supervises the stockroom clerk.
Richard Kozminski	Stockroom Clerk	Assists the stockroom supervisor. Unpacks new merchandise, and moves it to sales areas as necessary. Prepares merchandise for delivery to customers, and drives the delivery van.

1

Eleanor Chae	Cashier	Receives cash from customers and processes all charge account and bank credit card sales. Prepares the daily bank deposit and takes it to the bank. Handles the petty cash fund. Responsible for running the computer programs that provide a daily cash register summary and a daily inventory update.	You	Accountant	Maintains accounting records and files. Prepares financial statements and special reports, as requested by the owner. Issues checks to pay bills and maintains the checkbook. Reconciles the monthly bank statement. Assists the store's outside accounting firm with the annual audit.

ORGANIZATION CHART

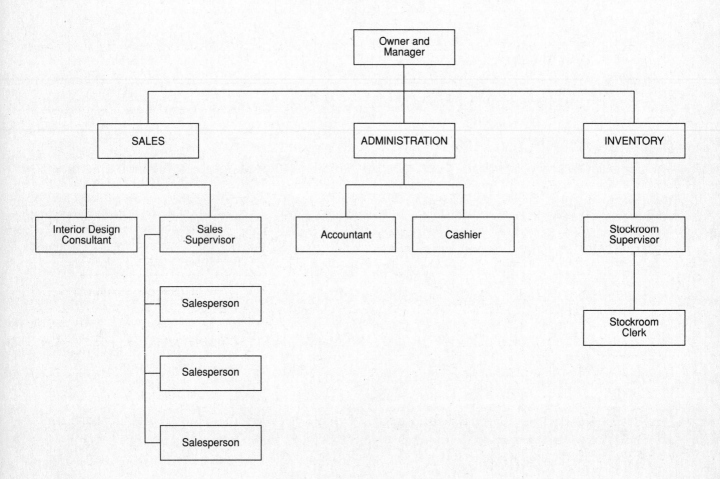

Figure 1

COMPANY PROCEDURES

The basic procedures that Wood n' Things uses to carry on its daily business activities are described in this section.

PURCHASING PROCEDURES

The purchasing procedures are as follows:

1. Wood n' Things utilizes its computer system to maintain its inventory records. (See Figure 2.) Data about purchases and sales are entered into the computer daily and the balance of each inventory item is updated daily. A report is generated by the computer at the end of each day listing any item that has fallen below a pre-established minimum quantity. The cashier notifies the owner that this item of stock must be replenished.

DAILY INVENTORY TRANSACTIONS

DATE	ORDER NO.	QUANTITY RECEIVED	QUANTITY SOLD	BALANCE
NO. 8-2468-21 DESK LAMP				
MAXIMUM 34 MINIMUM 10				
5/01/X5				12
5/03/X5			2	10
5/14/X5	PO 632	12		22
5/15/X5			4	18
5/17/X5			5	13
5/20/X5			3	10

Figure 2

2. The owner issues a purchase order to the manufacturer or wholesaler that handles the item. (See Figure 3.)

WOOD n'Things

TO Hi-Tech Manufacturing Co.
621 Broadway
New York, NY 10026-8243

PURCHASE ORDER NO. 653
DATE May 20, 19X5
SHIP VIA Fort Pitt Trucking Co.
TERMS 1/10, n/30
BY Amy Glenn

Quantity	Catalog No.	Description	Unit Price	Amount
24	8-2468-21	Desk Lamp	26 00	624 00

Figure 3

3. When the merchandise arrives, the stockroom clerk unpacks it, and the stockroom supervisor inspects it and fills out a receiving report. (See Figure 4.)

WOOD n'Things

RECEIVED FROM

Hi-Tech Manufacturing Company
621 Broadway
New York, NY 10026-8243

Receiving Report No. **A9491**

DATE RECEIVED
5/28/X5

PURCHASE ORDER NUMBER
PO 653

SHIPPER
Fort Pitt Trucking Co.

SHIPPED VIA
Truck

ACCEPTED BY
MW

QUANTITY RECEIVED	QUANTITY ACCEPTED	CATALOG NO.	DESCRIPTION
24	24	8-2468-21	Desk Lamp

Figure 4

4. The cashier, using the receiving report as documentation, enters the receipt of the merchandise into the computer inventory program. (See Figure 5.)

Figure 5

DAILY INVENTORY TRANSACTIONS   5/28/X5

DATE	ORDER NO.	QUANTITY RECEIVED	QUANTITY SOLD	BALANCE
NO. 8-2468-21 DESK LAMP				
MAXIMUM 34 MINIMUM 10				
5/01/X5				12
5/03/X5			2	10
5/14/X5	PO 632	12		22
5/15/X5			4	18
5/17/X5			5	13
5/20/X5			3	10
5/28/X5	PO 653	24		34

5. The owner prices the merchandise, and the stockroom supervisor attaches price tags to the individual items.

6. The stockroom clerk moves the merchandise to the designated area in the stockroom or to the appropriate sales area.

SALES PROCEDURES

The sales procedures are as follows.

1. A salesperson helps the customer to select merchandise and prepares a sales slip for the transaction.

2. The customer takes the sales slip to the store's cashier and either pays for the goods in cash, uses a bank credit card, or uses a credit card issued by Wood n' Things to people with charge accounts.

3. The cashier records the sale on the store's cash register. Wood n' Things has a modern electronic cash register system called a "store and forward" system. As individual transactions are entered each day, this system stores data about the transactions on a magnetic disk. At the end of the day, the disk is removed from the register and placed in the computer for processing. Thus, data is "forwarded" from the cash register system to the computer system. During the day, whenever a sale occurs, the cashier places the sales slip in a slot in the cash register and then records the following data about the sale: type of sale—cash, bank credit card, or charge account; customer number if a charge account sale; quantity and type of merchandise; and unit price. The cash register automatically extends the price and computes the sales tax and total price. This data, along with a description of the items sold, is printed on the sales slip by the cash register.

a. *Cash sales.* If the sale is for cash, the cashier will complete the transaction by collecting the cash and giving the customer a copy of the sales slip as a receipt.

b. *Bank credit card sales.* If the customer uses a bank credit card, credit authorization must be obtained before completing the transaction. The cashier passes the customer's card through a slot at the back of a small machine and enters the amount of the sale on the keyboard of the machine. This machine is connected electronically through a telephone line to the bank's credit card authorization department. An "electronic authorization" is relayed to the store's machine if the sale is acceptable. If it is, the cashier completes the transaction by using the customer's credit card to imprint the name and account number on a special credit card sales slip and by having the customer sign the sales slip. A copy of this sales slip and a copy of the store's own sales slip are given to the customer as a record of the transaction.

c. *Charge account sales.* If the customer is using a Wood n' Things credit card, the cashier will check the files to be sure the customer has a satisfactory credit standing. For sales over $500, the cashier must also obtain the owner's authorization before completing the sale. After verifying the customer's credit status, the cashier uses the customer's plastic Wood n' Things credit card to imprint the name and account number on the sales slip, has the customer sign the slip, and gives the customer a copy of the slip as a receipt.

4. If the customer requests home delivery, the cashier enters the necessary information on the sales slip and gives a copy to the stockroom supervisor, who arranges to have the stockroom clerk package and deliver the merchandise.

5. During the day, the cashier also uses the cash register to record cash collected from customers in settlement of their charge account balances. These amounts are received from the customers by mail and in person.

6. At the end of the day, the cashier removes the magnetic disk from the cash register and inserts it in the disk drive of the office computer. The disk drive is able to "read" the data stored on the disk. This data is then combined with file data from another disk and is processed by the computer system to produce a daily cash register summary.

The cash register summary lists all information about cash receipts in one section and all information about charge account sales in another section, as shown on Figure 6. Notice that there are three sources of cash receipts—cash sales, bank credit card sales, and collections on accounts receivable. The bank credit card sales are considered a source of cash receipts because the sales slips from these sales are taken to the bank with a special deposit slip each day, and the bank credits the total amount shown on the sales slips to the store's checking account as if it were a cash deposit. (At the end of the month, the bank deducts a fee for handling the credit card sales. This fee appears on the monthly bank statement that the firm receives.)

Figure 6

CASH REGISTER SUMMARY   05/29/X5

CASH RECEIPTS

CUSTOMER NO.	SOURCE	ACCTS. REC. COLLECTED	AMOUNT OF SALE FURNITURE & HOUSEWARES	SALES TAX	CASH RECEIVED
	CASH SALES		1950.00	117.00	2067.00
	BANK CREDIT CARD SALES		1280.00	76.80	1356.80
2984	ROSE DELANEY	400.00			400.00
6770	GEORGE SACHS	120.00			120.00
	TOTALS	520.00	3230.00	193.80	3943.80

CHARGE ACCOUNT SALES

CUSTOMER NO.	CUSTOMER NAME	AMOUNT OF SALE FURNITURE & HOUSEWARES	SALES TAX	TOTAL RECEIVABLE
4277	WILLIAM HUBBARD	2280.00	136.92	2416.92
6443	EDITH ROSS	361.00	21.91	382.91
	TOTALS	2641.00	158.83	2799.83

7. The magnetic disk taken from the cash register also contains data about the quantity and type of merchandise sold. The computer system uses this data to produce a daily summary of sales by item. This summary provides the information that the cashier needs to update the inventory to reflect the goods sold. A sample of a daily summary of sales by item is shown on Figure 7 below. The daily inventory update follows on Figure 8.

DAILY SUMMARY OF SALES BY ITEM   5/29/X5

STOCK NO.	ITEM	QUANTITY SOLD
4-9246-02	BOOKCASE	1
5-8872-24	FOLDING CHAIR	8
8-2468-21	DESK LAMP	2
9-1480-92	END TABLE	5

Figure 7

DAILY INVENTORY TRANSACTIONS   5/29/X5

DATE	ORDER NO.	QUANTITY RECEIVED	QUANTITY SOLD	BALANCE
NO. 8-2468-21 DESK LAMP				
MAXIMUM 34 MINIMUM 10				
5/01/X5				12
5/03/X5			2	10
5/14/X5	PO 632	12		22
5/15/X5			4	18
5/17/X5			5	13
5/20/X5			3	10
5/28/X5	PO 653	24		34
5/29/X5			2	32

      Figure 8

ACCOUNTING RECORDS

For the past two years you have been studying accounting at a local college. Ms. Glenn has asked you to begin working on June 1, 19X5, as the accountant for Wood n' Things, reporting to her. You have accepted the position.

Upon arriving for work on Monday, June 1, 19X5, you learn that the business has a fiscal year ending each June 30 and that your predecessor has journalized and posted all transactions through May 31 of the current fiscal year. You find that all records are up to date, were proved at the end of May, and are in good order. Ms. Glenn explains that you will have full responsibility for the checkbook, the five journals used, the general ledger, the subsidiary ledgers, and all other financial records and statements.

CHECKBOOK PROCEDURES

Recording Bank Deposits. All cash (including currency, coins, checks, and money orders) that the firm receives is processed by the cashier and deposited intact daily. The special sales slips for the bank credit card sales are also deposited each day. The bank's discount fee for handling these transactions is automatically deducted from the business's checking account at the end of the month, and the amount deducted is shown on the monthly bank statement.

The cashier prepares two bank deposit slips—one for the cash processed through the cash register and one for the bank credit card sales slips. Occasionally, there will also be other types of cash receipts transactions that will require the preparation of a bank deposit slip. When the cashier returns from the bank, she will give you the validated deposit slips so that you can enter the necessary data in the checkbook.

The procedures for recording bank deposits in the checkbook are as follows. (Refer to the checkbook illustration shown below as you read about these procedures.)

1. If necessary, bring forward the balance from the previous checkbook page and enter it in the "Bal. Bro't For'd" space. (Note: The June 1, 19X5, balance has been entered on the first page in your checkbook.)

2. Record the total amount of the deposit slip in the "Deposits" section of the check stub. Also enter the date of the deposit on the check stub to the left of the word "Deposits."

3. Compute the new balance of the checking account, and record it on the "Total" line.

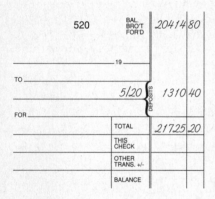

Issuing Checks. All expenditures of Wood n' Things, except petty cash payments, are made by check. The checks are prepared by you and signed by the owner.

The procedures for issuing checks and recording them in the checkbook are as follows. (Refer to the checkbook illustration shown below.)

1. Complete the check stub section first.

    a. If necessary, bring forward the balance from the previous checkbook page and enter the balance amount in the "Bal. Bro't For'd" space.

    b. Fill in the date, the name of the payee, and the reason for the payment on the check stub.

    c. Record the amount of the check on the "This Check" line.

    d. Compute the new balance of the checking account, and enter it on the "Balance" line.

    e. The "Other Trans. +/−" line is used to record transactions other than deposits and checks, such as Bank Service Charges.

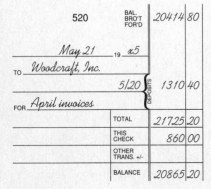

2. After you complete the check stub section, prepare the check itself.

    a. Enter the date at the top of the check.

    b. Enter the name of the payee after the words *Pay to the Order of.*

    c. Write the amount of the check in figures in the space to the right of the dollar sign.

    d. Write the dollar amount of the check in words on the line below the name of the payee. Use the word *and* to separate the dollar amount from the cents, and use a fraction for the cents, such as 25/100 for 25 cents. Use 00/100 if the check is for an even dollar amount. Draw a line from the fraction to the word *Dollars* in order to fill any empty space.

    e. Leave the signature line on the check blank. Only Amy Glenn is authorized to sign checks for the business.

    f. After you have written the check, remove it from the checkbook section and place it in the large envelope located on the inside of the back cover. In a real business situation you would forward all checks to Amy Glenn.

If you make an error when writing a check, void it by writing the word *Void* in large letters on both the check stub and the check. Use the next check to complete the transaction.

CASH RECEIPTS JOURNAL

At the close of business each day, the cashier uses the computer system to produce a daily cash register summary. These cash register summaries are located on pages 21-45 and can be removed for easier handling. You will record all the cash from cash sales, bank credit card sales, and accounts receivable collections listed on this summary in the cash receipts journal. Occasionally, there will also be other types of cash receipts transactions that must be entered in the cash receipts journal. After you have recorded the information from a summary, place it in the large envelope located on the inside of the back cover.

Credits to the customers' accounts in the accounts receivable subsidiary ledger are posted daily from the cash receipts journal. Items in the Other Accounts Credit column of this journal are posted at the end of each week. Summary postings of all column totals (except the total of the Other Accounts Credit column) are made at the end of the month.

Use 35 as the first page number for the cash receipts journal when you begin making entries. (Pages 1-34 were used to record the previous months' transactions.)

CASH PAYMENTS JOURNAL

You record all checks in the cash payments journal on a daily basis. Invoices and bills covering expenses are paid promptly upon receipt, and the transactions are entered in the cash payments journal immediately after the checks are prepared. Invoices covering purchases of merchandise for resale include a credit period and are therefore entered in the purchases journal when they are first received. These invoices are paid later in accordance with the credit terms, and the checks issued are then recorded in the cash payments journal. The cashier handles petty cash payments, which are periodically reimbursed by a check that you prepare. The amounts involved are recorded in the cash payments journal when the reimbursement check is issued.

Debits to the creditors' accounts in the accounts payable subsidiary ledger are posted daily from the cash payments journal. Items in the Other Accounts Debit column of this journal are posted at the end of each week. Summary postings of all column totals (except the total of the Other Accounts Debit column) are made at the end of the month.

Use 35 as the first page number for the cash payments journal when you begin making entries. (Pages 1-34 were used to record previous months' transactions.)

SALES JOURNAL

The cashier records all charge account sales on the cash register. The cash register summary prepared by the computer system each day lists these sales and provides the information that you need to enter them in the sales journal. Charge account customers normally have 30 days in which to pay. Cash discounts are not granted.

Each day you post from the sales journal to the customers' accounts in the accounts receivable subsidiary ledger. You make monthly summary postings of the column totals to the appropriate accounts in the general ledger.

Use 35 as the first page number for the sales journal when you begin making entries. (Pages 1-34 were used to record previous months' transactions.)

PURCHASES JOURNAL

The owner verifies all invoices received from suppliers and then gives you the invoices to record. You enter the credit

7

purchases of merchandise for resale in the purchases journal. After the necessary entries are made, you file the invoices by due date so that you can issue checks in a timely manner.

Each day you post from the purchases journal to the creditors' accounts in the accounts payable subsidiary ledger. You make monthly summary postings of the column totals to the appropriate general ledger accounts.

Use 35 as the first page number for the purchases journal when you begin making entries. (Page 1-34 were used to record previous months' transactions.)

GENERAL JOURNAL

Any transactions that cannot be recorded in the special journals are entered in the general journal. This journal is also used for adjusting, closing, and reversing entries at the end of the fiscal year.

You post from the general journal at the end of the week. Use 35 as the first page number for the general journal when you begin making entries. (Pages 1-34 were used to record previous months' transactions.)

GENERAL LEDGER

Balance-form ledger sheets are used for the general ledger accounts. The previous accountant prepared a trial balance as of May 31 to check the equality of the debits and credits in these accounts. The June 1 balances have been entered for your convenience. The chart of accounts is reproduced on page 91 for easy reference. (Note: Some of the accounts show no balances as of June 1.)

SUBSIDIARY LEDGERS

Wood n' Things has two subsidiary ledgers: an accounts receivable ledger and an accounts payable ledger.

Accounts Receivable Ledger. Accounts with individual customers are kept in alphabetical order on balance-form ledger sheets. The previous accountant proved this ledger against the Accounts Receivable account in the general ledger as of May 31. The June 1 balances have been entered for your convenience. Postings to this ledger are made daily from the sales journal and the cash receipts journal and weekly from the general journal.

Accounts Payable Ledger. Accounts with individual creditors are kept in alphabetical order using balance-form ledger sheets. The previous accountant proved this ledger against the Accounts Payable account in the general ledger as of May 31. The June 1 balances have been entered for your convenience. Postings to the accounts payable ledger are made daily from the purchases journal and the cash payments journal and weekly from the general journal.

SUMMARY OF ROUTINE ACCOUNTING PROCEDURES

The routine accounting procedures that you must perform for Wood n' Things during June are summarized below. The chart of accounts for the business appears on page 91.

DAILY PROCEDURES

The daily procedures include issuing checks, maintaining the checkbook, journalizing all transactions, and posting appropriate entries to the subsidiary ledgers. Daily postings ensure that the balances in the subsidiary ledger accounts are always current. As previously noted, the balances as of June 1 have already been entered in the ledgers. You are to begin your work with the recording of transactions for the month of June.

PAYROLL PROCEDURES

The full-time employees of Wood n' Things are paid semimonthly—on the 15th and the last business day of each month. Wood n' Things uses Payroll Systems Inc., an automated payroll service company, to handle most of its payroll functions. This company prepares the semimonthly payroll, prepares quarterly and year-end payroll tax returns, and keeps an individual earnings record for each employee. By using an outside service company to handle payroll work, Ms. Glenn has more time to devote to the operations of her business. In addition, the service company guarantees the accuracy of the payroll and relieves Ms. Glenn of the need to keep informed about changes in payroll tax rates and the requirements for filing payroll tax returns.

In its records, Payroll Systems Inc. has the name, address, marital status, number of withholding allowances, and hourly rate of each employee of Wood n' Things. Shortly before each payday, Ms. Glenn places a telephone call to the company to report the number of hours worked by each employee during the pay period. Payroll Systems Inc. then computes the gross earnings, deductions, and net pay for each employee; prepares a payroll register, a payroll summary, and payroll checks; and updates the employee earnings records. The company delivers the payroll register, summary, and checks the day before the employees are to be paid, and Ms. Glenn reviews all the documents for accuracy. She then signs the checks and distributes them to the employees.

For ease in maintaining its bank records, Wood n' Things uses a separate checking account just for payroll. Working from the payroll summary, you will issue a check from the regular checking account equal to the total net pay. This check will be deposited in the payroll account to cover the employees' individual paychecks. You will also use the payroll summary to journalize and post the accounting entries for payroll and payroll taxes.

END-OF-WEEK PROCEDURES

The routine procedures to be completed at the end of each week are outlined below.

1. Foot the amount columns in the cash receipts, cash payments, sales, and purchases journals. Enter the footings in small pencil figures immediately beneath the last line on which an entry has been made. Cross-foot to prove the equality of the debit and credit footings.

2. Determine the balance of the Cash account, and compare it with the checkbook balance. The procedure for determining the balance of the Cash account is as follows. Add the June 1 balance of the Cash account and the footing from the Cash Debit column of the cash receipts journal. From this total, subtract the footing of the Cash Credit column of the cash payments journal. Verify that the cash balance computed equals the checkbook balance. If the two amounts do not agree, check your work and correct any errors before proceeding.

3. Post all individual entries from the general journal and from the Other Accounts columns of the cash receipts journal and the cash payments journal to the general ledger.

4. Answer the Audit Check questions. Your instructor will indicate how you can determine the accuracy of your answers to these questions.

NARRATIVE OF TRANSACTIONS

The transactions that took place at Wood n' Things during June 19X5 are listed in this section. You are expected to record each transaction in the order given. The business papers that you will handle are copies of the daily cash register summary, which are given on pages 21-45. Refer to the appropriate summary form as necessary to complete your work. The other business papers that the accountant would normally receive are not included, but the essential data from them are given in the narrative of transactions. The checkbook, journals, ledgers, working papers, and statement forms that you will need are provided on pages 49-129.

MONDAY, JUNE 1

Trans. 1 Issue Check 529 for $350 to Chatham Realty in payment of the June garage rent.

Trans. 2 Issue Check 530 for $525 to Allegheny Electric Company for electricity used at the store during May.

Trans. 3 Received the daily cash register summary. Also received deposit slips totaling $1,359.54.

TUESDAY, JUNE 2

Trans. 4 Purchased merchandise from Butler Butcher Block Company for $12,890; terms 30 days net; Invoice 5449 dated May 29.

Trans. 5 Issue Check 531 for $380 to Tri-State Office Machines, Inc. for purchase of a fax machine.

Trans. 6 Received the daily cash register summary. Also received deposit slips totaling $2,460.51.

WEDNESDAY, JUNE 3

Trans. 7 Purchased merchandise from Carnegie Shelving Company for $1,867; terms 2/10, n/30; Invoice 12496 dated June 2.

Trans. 8 Issue Check 532 for $460 to *Pittsburgh Gazette* for May newspaper advertising.

Trans. 9 Received the daily cash register summary. Also received deposit slips totaling $2,677.51.

THURSDAY, JUNE 4

Trans. 10 Purchased merchandise from Danish Import Company for $3,833; terms 30 days net; Invoice 8964 dated June 1.

Trans. 11 Issue Check 533 for $5,286.80 to Oxford European Design, Inc. for May invoices.

Trans. 12 Issue Check 534 for $200 to Gray Hauling Company for May rubbish removal.

Trans. 13 Received the daily cash register summary. Also received deposit slips totaling $3,344.72.

FRIDAY, JUNE 5

Trans. 14 Issue Check 535 for $3,060 to First National Bank for deposit of amounts withheld from employees earnings for the semimonthly payroll period ended May 30 and employer's share of social security and medicare tax as follows:

Social Security Tax Withheld	$ 553
Medicare Tax Withheld	127
Federal Income Tax Withheld	1,700
Social Security Tax—Employer's Share	553
Medicare Tax—Employer's Share	127

Debit the payment of employer's share of payroll taxes to Payroll Taxes Payable.

Trans. 15 Issue Check 536 for $1,255.38 to Carnegie Shelving Company for a May invoice less the 2 percent discount. (Refer to the creditor's account to find the full amount of the invoice.)

Trans. 16 Issue Check 537 for $825 to Highland Insurance Agency to pay the premium for a one-year fire insurance policy.

Trans. 17 Received the daily cash register summary. Also received deposit slips totaling $1,485.06.

SATURDAY, JUNE 6

Trans. 18 Received the daily cash register summary. Also received deposit slips totaling $1,787.16.

END-OF-WEEK PROCEDURES

Complete the end-of-week procedures. See top of this page.

AUDIT CHECK:

1. Checkbook balance should be $21,859.50.
2. How much does Wood n' Things owe Carnegie Shelving Company as of June 6? _1867⁰⁰_
3. What were the total credit sales for the week ended June 6? _12,771⁰⁰_
4. Check No. 531 to Tri-State Office Machines, Inc. was posted to what account? _____ _Office Supplies_

MONDAY, JUNE 8

Trans. 19 Issue Check 538 for $3,252.15 to Hi-Tech Manufacturing Company for a May invoice less the 1 percent discount (Refer to the creditor's account to find the full amount of the invoice.)

Trans. 20 Issue Check 539 for $192.50 to Fort Pitt Trucking Company for freight charges on purchases from J & K Designs.

Trans. 21 Issue Check 540 for $210 to Pennsylvania Telephone Company for the monthly telephone bill.

Trans. 22 Received the daily cash register summary. Also received deposit slips totaling $6,741.74.

TUESDAY, JUNE 9

Trans. 23 Purchased merchandise from Oxford European Design, Inc., for $1,417; terms 30 days net; Invoice 6098 dated June 5.

Trans. 24 Purchased merchandise from Woodcraft, Inc. for $1,715; terms 30 days net; Invoice 809 dated June 8.

Trans. 25 Issue Check 541 for $3,570 to Pennsylvania State Department of Revenue for sales tax collected during May.

Trans. 26 Received the daily cash register summary. Also received deposit slips totaling $4,375.08.

WEDNESDAY, JUNE 10

Trans. 27 Issue Check 542 for $275 to Western Oil Company for gasoline used in the delivery van.

Trans. 28 Received a check from Highland Insurance Agency for $100 as a refund for overpayment of the fire insurance premium paid on June 5.

Trans. 29 Received the daily cash register summary. Also received deposit slips totaling $3,031.24. (This amount includes the refund for overpayment of the insurance premium.)

THURSDAY, JUNE 11

Trans. 30 Purchased merchandise from Nordic Furniture Company for $2,982; terms 2/10, n/30; Invoice 6409 dated June 9.

Trans. 31 Issue Check 543 for $14,129.60 to Butler Butcher Block Company for May invoices.

Trans. 32 Received Credit Memorandum 211 for $527 from Oxford European Design, Inc., for damaged furniture that was returned. The furniture was purchased on Invoice 6098 dated June 5.

Trans. 33 Received the daily cash register summary. Also received deposit slips totaling $2,123.60.

FRIDAY, JUNE 12

Trans. 34 Issue Check 544 for $510 to Pennsylvania Department of Revenue for state income tax withheld from employee earnings during May.

Trans. 35 Issue Check 545 for $1,829.66 to Carnegie Shelving Company for Invoice 12496 dated June 2 less 2 percent discount.

Trans. 36 Received the daily cash register summary. Also received deposit slips totaling $2,007.64.

SATURDAY, JUNE 13

Trans. 37 Received the daily cash register summary. Also received deposit slips totaling $4,315.26.

END-OF-WEEK PROCEDURES

Complete the end-of-week procedures.

AUDIT CHECK:

1. Checkbook balance should be $20,485.15.
2. Check No. 537 to Highland Insurance Agency was posted to what account?
   Prepaid Insurance
3. How much does Jean Alvarez owe Wood n' Things as of June 13?
   $1211.38
4. How much does Wood n' Things owe Oxford European Design, Inc. as of June 13?
   $890.00

MONDAY, JUNE 15

Trans. 38 Record the semimonthly payroll.
   1. Make a general journal entry to record the total payroll for June 1-15. The payroll summary provided by the automated payroll service company is shown below.

PAYROLL SYSTEMS INC.

PAYROLL SUMMARY

COMPANY NAME: WOOD n' THINGS
PAY PERIOD ENDING: JUNE 15, 19X5

DEPT. NO.	DEPARTMENT	GROSS EARNINGS	DEDUCTIONS				NET PAY
			SOCIAL SECURITY	MEDICARE TAX	FEDERAL INC. TAX	STATE INC. TAX	
601	SALES	6,000	390	90	1,400	180	3,940
602	OFFICE	1,540	100	23	230	46	1,141
603	STOCKROOM	1,230	80	18	185	37	910
	TOTALS	8,770	570	131	1,815	263	5,991

a. The business has separate expense accounts for sales, office, and stockroom salaries. The payroll summary lists the gross earnings by departments. Debit the amount for each department to the appropriate expense account.

b. Credit the total of each deduction to the appropriate liability account.

c. Credit the total net pay to Salaries Payable.

2. Make a general journal entry to record the employer's social security and medicare tax liability of $701 (sum of employer's matching share of social security withheld of $570 and medicare withheld of $131). Debit Payroll Taxes Expense and credit Payroll Taxes Payable in accordance with the established procedure used at Wood n' Things. (An alternative accounting procedure is to credit the specific tax liability accounts.)

3. Issue Check 546 for the total net pay to Wood n' Things Payroll account in order to transfer the necessary funds from the regular checking account. Enter this check in the cash payments journal, with the amount debited to Salaries Payable in the Other Accounts Debit column.

Trans. 39 Issue Check 547 for $1,700 to Amy Glenn, the owner, as a withdrawal for personal living expenses. Ms. Glenn makes a similar withdrawal at the end of each payroll period.

Trans. 40 Received the daily cash register summary. Also received deposit slips totaling $2,119.29.

TUESDAY, JUNE 16

Trans. 41 Purchased merchandise from Butler Butcher Block Company for $4,984; terms 30 days net; Invoice 8902 dated June 11.

Trans. 42 Issue Check 548 for $5,814 to Danish Import Company for a May invoice due tomorrow.

Trans. 43 Received the daily cash register summary. Also received deposit slips totaling $941.28.

WEDNESDAY, JUNE 17

Trans. 44 Purchased merchandise from Nordic Furniture Company for $2,021; terms 2/10, n/30; Invoice 9920 dated June 15.

Trans. 45 Issue Check 549 for $2,000 to J & K Designs to apply on account.

Trans. 46 Gave Credit Memorandum 105 for $20 to James Dolan, a charge account customer, for damaged merchandise sold to him on June 15. (NOTE: Do not debit Sales Tax Payable in connection with this transaction. When Wood n' Things grants an allowance for damaged goods, the firm absorbs the total loss, including the sales tax. This practice is good for customer relations.)

Trans. 47 Received the daily cash register summary. Also received deposit slips totaling $2,034.92.

THURSDAY, JUNE 18

Trans. 48 Purchased merchandise from Danish Import Company for $3,529; terms 30 days net; Invoice 9113 dated June 16.

Trans. 49 Issue Check 550 for $178.25 to Manchester Freight Company for freight charges on furniture purchased from Butler Butcher Block Company.

Trans. 50 Issue Check 551 for $2,922.36 to Nordic Furniture Company for Invoice 6409 less the 2 percent discount.

Trans. 51 Received a check for $10,600 from North Side Savings and Loan Association because a short-term investment in a certificate of deposit matured. The principal (face value) of the certificate of deposit was $10,000 and the interest earned was $600.

Trans. 52 Received the daily cash register summary. Also received deposit slips totaling $11,886.84. (This amount includes the principal and interest from the certificate of deposit that matured.)

FRIDAY, JUNE 19

Trans. 53 Issue Check 552 for $3,217 to First National Bank for deposit of amounts withheld from employees earnings for the semimonthly payroll period ended June 15 and employer's share of social security and medicare tax as follows:

Social Security Tax Withheld	$ 570
Medicare Tax Withheld	131
Federal Income Tax Withheld	1,815
Social Security Tax—Employer's Share	570
Medicare Tax—Employer's Share	131

Debit the payment of employer's share of payroll taxes to Payroll Taxes Payable.

Trans. 54 Issue Check 553 for $1,560 to Monroeville Savings and Loan Association for the monthly payment of $600 principal and $960 interest due on the mortgage on the store building.

Trans. 55 Received Credit Memorandum 1863 for $250 from Nordic Furniture Company as an allowance to compensate for the shipment of chairs in the wrong color. These chairs were purchased on Invoice 9920 dated June 15.

Trans. 56 Received the daily cash register summary. Also received deposit slips totaling $1,841.22.

SATURDAY, JUNE 20

Trans. 57 Received the daily cash register summary. Also received deposit slips totaling $1,951.46.

END-OF-WEEK-PROCEDURES

Complete the end-of-week procedures.

AUDIT CHECK:

1. Checkbook balance should be $17,877.55.
2. What is the balance of the Short-Term Investments account as of June 20?

$10,000

11

3. How much does James Dolan owe Wood n' Things as of June 20?

$334.67

4. What is the balance of the Payroll Taxes Payable account as of June 20?

0

MONDAY, JUNE 22

Trans. 58 Issue Check 554 for $3,833 to Danish Import Company for Invoice 8964 dated June 1.

Trans. 59 Purchased merchandise from Nordic Furniture Company for $3,924; terms 2/10, n/30; Invoice 9987 dated June 19.

Trans. 60 The account receivable of $112.87 owed by James Tashiko appears to be uncollectible, and the owner has instructed that it is to be written off. (The firm uses the allowance method to write off uncollectible accounts.)

Trans. 61 Received the daily cash register summary. Also received deposit slips totaling $1,926.87.

TUESDAY, JUNE 23

Trans. 62 Issue Check 555 for $890 to Oxford European Design, Inc., for Invoice 6098 dated June 5 less Credit Memorandum 211.

Trans. 63 Received the daily cash register summary. Also received deposit slips totaling $2,012.51.

WEDNESDAY, JUNE 24

Trans. 64 Purchased merchandise from Carnegie Shelving Company for $1,483; terms 2/10, n/30; Invoice 20249 dated June 22.

Trans. 65 Issue Check 556 for $1,735.58 to Nordic Furniture Company for Invoice 9920 dated June 15 less Credit Memorandum 1863 and the 2 percent discount.

Trans. 66 Received the daily cash register summary. Also received deposit slips totaling $5,054.08.

THURSDAY, JUNE 25

Trans. 67 Issue Check 557 for $110 to William Sloan, attorney, as a legal fee for his efforts to collect an overdue account.

Trans. 68 Received the daily cash register summary. Also received deposit slips totaling $3,336.88.

FRIDAY, JUNE 26

Trans. 69 Purchased merchandise from Oxford European Design, Inc., for $621; terms 30 days net; Invoice 8821 dated June 23.

Trans. 70 Gave Credit Memorandum 106 for $97.52 to Kim Lee, a charge account customer, for a return of merchandise sold to her on June 23. DO NOT DEBIT SALES TAX PAYABLE.

Trans. 71 Issue Check 558 for $92 to Western Oil Company for gasoline used in the delivery van.

Trans. 72 Received the daily cash register summary. Also received deposit slips totaling $1,705.54.

SATURDAY, JUNE 27

Trans. 73 Received the daily cash register summary. Also received deposit slips totaling $1,499.90. NOTE: Since there are only two more business days in this month, defer the end-of-week procedures until the close of business on Tuesday, June 30.

MONDAY, JUNE 29

Trans. 74 Issue Check 559 for $12,890 to Butler Butcher Block Company for Invoice 5449 dated May 29.

Trans. 75 Issue Check 560 for $5,040 to First National Bank to repay a 30-day note payable dated May 29. The principal is $5,000 and the interest is $40.

Trans. 76 Received the daily cash register summary. Also received deposit slips totaling $1,704.48.

TUESDAY, JUNE 30

Trans. 77 Record the semimonthly payroll. Make the general journal entries to record the June 16-30 payroll and the employer's social security and medicare tax liability. Issue Check 561 for the total net pay to Wood n' Things Payroll Account. Enter this check in the cash payments journal, debiting Salaries Payable in the Other Accounts Debit column. Obtain the necessary information from the payroll summary shown below.

PAYROLL SYSTEMS INC.

PAYROLL SUMMARY

COMPANY NAME: WOOD n' THINGS
PAY PERIOD ENDING: JUNE 30, 19X5

| DEPT. NO. | DEPARTMENT | GROSS EARNINGS | DEDUCTIONS | | | | NET PAY |
			SOCIAL SECURITY	MEDICARE TAX	FEDERAL INC. TAX	STATE INC. TAX	
601	SALES	6,200	403	93	1,426	186	4,092
602	OFFICE	1,480	96	22	222	44	1,096
603	STOCKROOM	1,230	80	18	185	37	910
	TOTALS	8,910	579	133	1,833	267	6,098

Trans. 78 Issue Check 562 for $1,700 to Amy Glenn as her withdrawal for the payroll period.

Trans. 79 Issue Check 563 for $46 to Eleanor Chae, cashier, to reimburse the petty cash fund for the following expenditures:

Store Supplies	$11
Office Supplies	12
Delivery Expense	23
	$46

Trans. 80 Received the daily cash register summary. Also received deposit slips totaling $3,078.66.

END-OF-WEEK PROCEDURES

Complete the end-of-week procedures.

AUDIT CHECK:

1. Checkbook balance should be $5,761.89.
2. What is the balance of the Allowance for Uncollectible Accounts account as of June 30?

   $155.13

3. Check No. 563 to reimburse the Petty Cash Fund was debited to what account(s)?

   Office Supplies, Store Supplies?

4. How much does Wood n' Things owe Nordic Furniture Company as of June 30?

   $3924

MONTHLY PROCEDURES

RECONCILING THE BANK STATEMENT

Complete the following monthly procedures.

The June bank statement received by Wood n' Things is shown below. Use the two-column analysis paper given on page 75 to prepare a bank reconciliation as follows.

First National Bank
Pittsburgh, PA

Wood n' Things
3308 Walnut Street
Pittsburgh, PA 15232

ACCOUNT NUMBER   043000261

PERIOD ENDING   June 30, 19X5

Checks	Checks	Checks	Deposits	Date	Balance
				June 1	21,087.18
			1,359.54	2	22,446.72
			2,460.51	3	24,907.23
			2,677.51	4	27,059.74
525.00			3,344.72	5	30,054.46
350.00			1,485.06	8	27,654.52
825.00	3,060.00		1,787.16	8	29,441.68
			6,741.74	9	30,896.62
5,286.80			4,375.00	10	34,091.70
380.00			3,031.24	11	37,252.94
210.00	460.00		2,123.60	12	34,551.16
3,570.00	1,255.38		2,007.64	15	18,667.05
3,252.15	510.00	14,129.60	4,315.26	15	22,982.31
			2,119.29	16	23,401.60
1,700.00			941.28	17	18,076.88
5,991.00	275.00		2,034.92	18	20,111.80
			11,886.84	19	30,168.98
1,829.66			1,841.22	22	25,870.84
2,922.36	3,217.00		1,951.46	22	27,822.30
			1,926.87	23	23,742.67
5,814.00	192.50		2,012.51	24	22,195.18
2,000.00	1,560.00		5,054.08	25	27,249.26
			3,336.88	26	28,740.56
1,735.58	110.00		1,705.54	29	26,521.10
92.00	3,833.00		1,499.90	29	28,021.00
			1,704.48	30	11,622.17
5,040.00	12,890.00	173.31 SC			

Beginning Balance	Total Amount of Deposits	Total Amount of Checks Paid	Total Charges	Ending Balance
21,087.18	73,724.33	83,016.03	173.31	11,622.17

	Number of Deposits Made	Number of Checks Paid	Number of Other Charges	
	25	29	1	

Codes:	CC Certified Check	OD Overdrawn	Please examine this statement upon receipt and report at once if you find any
	DM Debit Memorandum	RI Returned Item	difference. If no error is reported in ten days, the account will be considered
	EC Error Correction	SC Service Charge	correct. All items are subject to final payment.
	BB Bank Transfer		

1. Record the balance for June 30, 19X5 shown on the bank statement.
2. Since the firm deposits all of its cash receipts intact on a daily basis, compare the total cash receipts for each day listed in the checkbook to the deposits listed on the bank statement. Place check marks next to the checkbook amounts that agree with the reported deposits. List on the reconciliation any deposit not shown on the bank statement and add the total deposits in transit to the bank balance.
3. Compare the checks listed in the checkbook with those that appear on the bank statement. Place check marks beside the amounts in the checkbook to show which amounts agree. List on the reconciliation the numbers and amounts of any checks that have not yet been paid by the bank. Subtract the total outstanding checks from the bank balance.
4. Place double rules under the adjusted bank balance.
5. Record the checkbook balance as of June 30, 19X5.
6. List the service charge deducted by the bank for processing bank credit card transactions. Subtract this amount from the book balance.
7. Place double rules under the adjusted book balance. This amount should agree with the adjusted bank balance. If it does not, verify your work before proceeding.

Record the bank service charge in the checkbook. Enter the amount of the service charge on the "Other Trans. + / − " line after the last check written. Put parentheses around the amount to indicate that the service charge amount is to be subtracted from the balance. Then compute the new cash balance by subtracting the service charge from the previous balance.

In addition, record the bank service charge as a "noncheck" entry in the cash payments journal. Debit Discount Expense on Bank Credit Card Sales, and credit Cash. Post the debit entry to the appropriate general ledger account. Foot the amount columns in the cash payments journal again. Enter the footings in small pencil figures, and cross-foot to prove the equality of the debit and credit amounts.

END-OF-MONTH PROCEDURES

All regular transactions for the month of June have now been recorded. Complete the following end-of-month procedures.
1. Since the footings have been entered and proved in each special journal, total and rule these journals.
2. Verify that all individual postings to the general ledger have been made from the general journal and the Other Accounts columns of the cash receipts and cash payments journals.
3. Make the required summary postings of the column totals from the special journals (except the totals of the Other Accounts columns) to the proper general ledger accounts.
4. Prepare a schedule of accounts receivable as of June 30, 19X5, and prove the total by comparing it with the balance of the Accounts Receivable account ($15,909.13). If the two amounts do not agree, check your work before proceeding.
5. Prepare a schedule of accounts payable as of June 30, 19X5, and prove the total by comparing it with the balance of the Accounts Payable account ($19,352.50). If the two amounts do not agree, check your work before proceeding.
6. Prepare a trial balance to prove the accuracy of the general ledger accounts as of June 30, 19X5. Use the ten-column worksheet. This will enable you to save time in completing the end-of-year procedures. List the titles of all general ledger accounts, including Income Summary 399, whether or not the accounts have balances. Verify the equality of the debit and credit totals. If these totals are not equal ($1,124,950.72), check your work before proceeding.

END-OF-YEAR PROCEDURES

The fiscal year of Wood n' Things ends on June 30. You are now ready to perform the necessary end-of-year procedures.

THE WORKSHEET AND FINANCIAL STATEMENTS

1. Record the following adjustments on the worksheet.
   a-b. Enter the adjustments for merchandise inventory on the worksheet. The ending merchandise inventory is $62,738. Use the letters a and b for these adjustments.
   c. The loss from uncollectible accounts is estimated at 1/2 of 1 percent of net credit sales. An analysis of the year's sales shows net credit sales to be $213,698. Make an adjustment for the estimated loss from uncollectible accounts. Use the letter c to identify this adjustment.
   d. On April 1, 19X5, Wood n' Things purchased a one-year, $10,000 U.S. Treasury note that has an interest rate of 6 percent. The firm will receive the interest in cash at the end of each six-month period. Therefore it is necessary to accrue the interest earned for April, May and June 19X5. Use the letter d to identify this adjustment. (Use the formula Principal x Rate x Time to compute the accrued interest.)
   e. Analysis of the firm's insurance policies shows that $3,145 of the premiums currently recorded in the Prepaid Insurance account represents coverage that has expired. Record an adjustment for the expired amount. Use the letter e to identify this adjustment.
   f. A physical inventory of the store supplies shows items totaling $480 on hand as of June 30. Make an adjustment for the store supplies used during the fiscal year. Identify this adjustment with the letter f.
   g. A physical inventory of the office supplies shows items totaling $170 on hand as of June 30. Make an adjustment for the office supplies used during the fiscal year. Identify this adjustment with the letter g.

h. The firm's depreciation schedules show that the following amounts of depreciation should be taken for the fiscal year ended June 30, 19X5: building, $12,000; store fixtures and equipment, $4,830; and delivery equipment, $900. Use the letter *h* to identify the adjustment for depreciation. Since the firm uses a single depreciation expense account, add the three depreciation amounts and debit the total to this account. Credit the appropriate Accumulated Depreciation accounts for the individual depreciation amounts.

i. The firm owes $1,957 of federal and state unemployment taxes for the quarter ended June 30. Record an adjustment for these accrued taxes. Credit Payroll Taxes Payable for the amount. Use the letter *i* to identify the adjustment. (It is not necessary to accrue the employer's share of the Social Security and Medicare tax, since the liability for these taxes was recorded as part of the semimonthly payroll entries.)

j. The balance in the Notes Payable account represents a $5,000, six-month note with an interest rate of 9 percent, which was signed on May 1, 19X5. Make an adjustment for the interest that has accrued from the date the note was issued until June 30. Identify this adjustment with the letter *j*.

2. Foot the figures in the Adjustment columns of the worksheet, verify the equality of the debit and credit totals, and then enter the totals and rule the columns.

3. Complete the Adjusted Trial Balance section. Combine the trial balance figures and the adjustments and extend the resulting amounts into the Adjusted Trial Balance columns. Foot and prove these columns, verify the equality of the debit and credit totals, enter the totals, and rule the columns.

4. Complete the Income Statement and Balance Sheet sections.

   a. Extend the balances of the asset, liability, and owner's equity accounts to the Balance Sheet columns.

   b. Extend the balances of the revenue, cost, and expense accounts to the Income Statement columns.

   c. Foot the figures in the four columns, determine the net income and transfer it from the Income Statement section to the Balance Sheet section. The net income should be $87,402.38.

   d. Enter the subtotals, bring down the final totals in all columns, verify the equality of the debit and credit totals, and rule the columns.

5. Prepare an income statement for the fiscal year ended June 30, 19X5. The income statement from the previous fiscal year is illustrated below and on page 16. Use it as a guide. The $87,402.38 net income for the year computed on the worksheet must agree with the net income for the period as shown on the income statement.

WOOD n' THINGS
INCOME STATEMENT
YEAR ENDED JUNE 30, 19X4

Operating Revenue

Sales		$722,131.00	
Less Sales Returns and Allowances		15,548.00	
Net Sales			$706,583.00

Cost of Goods Sold

Merchandise Inventory, July 1, 19X3		$ 68,306.00	
Merchandise Purchases	$424,410.58		
Freight In	15,745.00		
Delivered Cost of Purchases	$440,155.58		
Less Purchases Returns and Allowances	$6,870.00		
Purchases Discounts	5,629.05	12,499.05	
Net Delivered Cost of Purchases		427,656.53	
Total Merchandise Available for Sale		$495,962.53	
Less Merchandise Inventory, June 30, 19X4		67,862.00	
Cost of Goods Sold			428,100.53

Gross Profit on Sales			$278,482.47

Operating Expenses

Sales Salaries Expense	$ 66,260.00	
Office Salaries Expense	30,967.00	
Stockroom Salaries Expense	24,580.00	
Payroll Taxes Expense	13,260.00	
Rent Expense—Garage	4,680.00	
Utilities Expense	8,610.28	
Telephone Expense	1,470.00	
Store Supplies Expense	1,482.00	

Operating Expenses (continued)

Office Supplies Expense	752.68	
Delivery Expense	6,535.18	
Advertising Expense	2,081.00	
Rubbish Removal Expense	2,100.00	
Insurance Expense	3,265.00	
Loss from Uncollectible Accounts	1,208.14	
Accounting and Legal Expense	7,260.00	
Discount Expense on Bank Credit Card Sales	1,892.14	
Depreciation Expense	18,600.00	
Total Operating Expenses		195,003.42
Net Income from Operations		$ 83,479.05
Other Income		
Interest Income	$ 2,482,00	
Other Expenses		
Interest Expense	10,492.00	
Net Nonoperating Expense		8,010.00
Net Income for Year		$75,469.05

6. Prepare a statement of owner's equity for the fiscal year
   ended June 30, 19X5. The owner made no additional
   investments during the year.

WOOD n' THINGS
STATEMENT OF OWNER'S EQUITY
YEAR ENDED JUNE 30, 19X4

Amy Glenn, Capital, July 1, 19X3		$105,677.98
Net Income for Year	$ 75,469.05	
Less Withdrawals for the Year	30,000.00	
Increase in Capital		45,469.05
Amy Glenn, Capital, June 30, 19X4		$151,147.03

7. Prepare a classified balance sheet in report form as of June
   30, 19X5. A copy of the previous year's balance sheet
   appears below and on page 17.

WOOD n' THINGS
BALANCE SHEET
JUNE 30, 19X4

Assets
Current Assets

Cash		$ 5,119.61
Petty Cash Fund		50.00
Short-Term Investments		5,000.00
Accounts Receivable	$ 12,409.69	
Less Allowance for Uncollectible Accounts	578.12	11,831.57
Interest Receivable		150.00
Merchandise Inventory		67,862.00

Current Assets (continued)

Prepaid Expenses			
Prepaid Insurance	$ 1,826.00		
Store Supplies	642.00		
Office Supplies	276.00	2,744.00	
Total Current Assets			$ 92,757.18

Plant and Equipment

Land		$ 20,000.00	
Building	$240,000.00		
Less Accumulated Depreciation	60,000.00	180,000.00	
Store Fixtures and Equipment	$ 32,000.00		
Less Accumulated Depreciation	22,000.00	10,000.00	
Delivery Equipment	$ 9,000.00		
Less Accumulated Depreciation	7,200.00	1,800.00	
Total Plant and Equipment			211,800.00
Total Assets			$304,557.18

Liabilities and Owner's Equity

Current Liabilities

Notes Payable	$ 25,000.00	
Accounts Payable	41,870.63	
Social Security Tax Payable	528.00	
Medicare Tax Payable	124.00	
Federal Income Tax Payable	1,184.00	
State Income Tax Payable	243.00	
Payroll Taxes Payable	1,847.00	
Sales Tax Payable	3,187.52	
Interest Payable	26.00	
Total Current Liabilities		$ 74,010.15

Long-Term Liabilities

Mortgage Payable		79,400.00
Total Liabilities		$153,410.15

Owner's Equity

Amy Glenn, Capital		151,147.03
Total Liabilities and Owner's Equity		$304,557.18

ADJUSTING AND CLOSING PROCEDURES

You are now ready to complete the adjusting and closing procedures.

1. In the general journal, record the adjusting entries for the accounting period.
2. Post the adjusting entries to the general ledger.
3. In the general journal, close the revenue and other temporary accounts with credit balances except the Income Summary account.
4. In the general journal, close the expense accounts and other temporary accounts with debit balances except the Income Summary account.
5. Post the first two closing entries to the general ledger.
6. In the general journal, record the entry to transfer the net income to the owner's capital account.
7. In the general journal, record the entry to close the owner's drawing account.
8. Post the last two closing entries to the general ledger.
9. Prepare a postclosing trial balance as of June 30, 19X5. Make sure that the debit and credit totals are equal.
10. In the general journal, record any reversing entries that may be necessary. Date these entries July 1, 19X5.
11. Post the reversing entries to the general ledger.

NOTE: Your instructor will indicate which materials you are to submit.

CASH REGISTER SUMMARIES

CASH REGISTER SUMMARY

CASH COLLECTIONS

CUSTOMER NO.	SOURCE	ACCTS. REC. COLLECTED	AMOUNT OF SALE	SALES TAX	CASH RECEIVED
	CASH SALES		1210.00	72.60	1282.60
	BANK CREDIT CARD SALES				
9672	ARNOLD WEXLER	76.94			76.94
	TOTALS	76.94	1210.00	72.60	1359.54

CHARGE ACCOUNT SALES

CUSTOMER NO.	CUSTOMER NAME	AMOUNT OF SALE	SALES TAX	TOTAL RECEIVABLE
6770	GEORGE SACHS	110.00	6.60	116.60
	TOTALS	110.00	6.60	116.60

CASH REGISTER SUMMARY

CASH COLLECTIONS

CUSTOMER NO.	SOURCE	ACCTS. REC. COLLECTED	AMOUNT OF SALE	SALES TAX	CASH RECEIVED
	CASH SALES		1960.00	117.60	2077.60
	BANK CREDIT CARD SALES				
6443	EDITH ROSS	382.91			382.91
	TOTALS	382.91	1960.00	117.60	2460.51

CHARGE ACCOUNT SALES

CUSTOMER NO.	CUSTOMER NAME	AMOUNT OF SALE	SALES TAX	TOTAL RECEIVABLE
1089	JEAN ALVAREZ	876.00	52.56	928.56
	TOTALS	876.00	52.56	928.56

CASH REGISTER SUMMARY

06/03/X5

CASH COLLECTIONS

CUSTOMER NO.	SOURCE	ACCTS. REC. COLLECTED	AMOUNT OF SALE	SALES TAX	CASH RECEIVED
	CASH SALES		2145.00	128.70	2273.70
	BANK CREDIT CARD SALES				
9864	HENRY ZACCARELLI	403.81			403.81
	TOTALS	403.81	2145.00	128.70	2677.51

CHARGE ACCOUNT SALES

CUSTOMER NO.	CUSTOMER NAME	AMOUNT OF SALE	SALES TAX	TOTAL RECEIVABLE
2984	ROSE DELANEY	715.00	42.90	757.90
	TOTALS	715.00	42.90	757.90

CASH REGISTER SUMMARY

06/04/X5

CASH COLLECTIONS

CUSTOMER NO.	SOURCE	ACCTS. REC. COLLECTED	AMOUNT OF SALE	SALES TAX	CASH RECEIVED
	CASH SALES		1758.00	105.48	1863.48
	BANK CREDIT CARD SALES		454.00	27.24	481.24
6846	JOHN SCHUETZ	1000.00			1000.00
	TOTALS	1000.00	2212.00	132.72	3344.72

CHARGE ACCOUNT SALES

CUSTOMER NO.	CUSTOMER NAME	AMOUNT OF SALE	SALES TAX	TOTAL RECEIVABLE
	TOTALS			

CASH REGISTER SUMMARY

06/05/X5

CASH COLLECTIONS

CUSTOMER NO.	SOURCE	ACCTS. REC. COLLECTED	AMOUNT OF SALE	SALES TAX	CASH RECEIVED
	CASH SALES		1401.00	84.06	1485.06
	BANK CREDIT CARD SALES				
	TOTALS		1401.00	84.06	1485.06

CHARGE ACCOUNT SALES

CUSTOMER NO.	CUSTOMER NAME	AMOUNT OF SALE	SALES TAX	TOTAL RECEIVABLE
3118	JAMES DOLAN	56.00	3.36	59.36
6281	MIRIAM RIGROSKI	400.00	24.00	424.00
	TOTALS	456.00	27.36	483.36

CASH REGISTER SUMMARY

06/06/X5

CASH COLLECTIONS

CUSTOMER NO.	SOURCE	ACCTS. REC. COLLECTED	AMOUNT OF SALE	SALES TAX	CASH RECEIVED
	CASH SALES		480.00	28.80	508.80
	BANK CREDIT CARD SALES		1206.00	72.36	1278.36
	TOTALS		1686.00	101.16	1787.16

CHARGE ACCOUNT SALES

CUSTOMER NO.	CUSTOMER NAME	AMOUNT OF SALE	SALES TAX	TOTAL RECEIVABLE
	TOTALS			

CASH REGISTER SUMMARY

06/08/X5

CASH COLLECTIONS

CUSTOMER NO.	SOURCE	ACCTS. REC. COLLECTED	AMOUNT OF SALE	SALES TAX	CASH RECEIVED
	CASH SALES		1862.00	111.72	1973.72
	BANK CREDIT CARD SALES				
4277	WILLIAM HUBBARD	500.00			500.00
7649	CAROL THOMPSON	4268.02			4268.02
	TOTALS	4768.02	1862.00	111.72	6741.74

CHARGE ACCOUNT SALES

CUSTOMER NO.	CUSTOMER NAME	AMOUNT OF SALE	SALES TAX	TOTAL RECEIVABLE
6770	GEORGE SACHS	385.00	23.10	408.10
6907	STEPHEN SIDORSKY	230.00	13.80	243.80
	TOTALS	615.00	36.90	651.90

CASH REGISTER SUMMARY

06/09/X5

CASH COLLECTIONS

CUSTOMER NO.	SOURCE	ACCTS. REC. COLLECTED	AMOUNT OF SALE	SALES TAX	CASH RECEIVED
	CASH SALES		2358.00	141.48	2499.48
	BANK CREDIT CARD SALES		839.00	50.34	889.34
2745	MAX BUKOWSKI	986.26			986.26
	TOTALS	986.26	3197.00	191.82	4375.08

CHARGE ACCOUNT SALES

CUSTOMER NO.	CUSTOMER NAME	AMOUNT OF SALE	SALES TAX	TOTAL RECEIVABLE
4316	SYLVIA GERBER	56.00	3.36	59.36
	TOTALS	56.00	3.36	59.36

CASH REGISTER SUMMARY

06/10/X5

CASH COLLECTIONS

CUSTOMER NO.	SOURCE	ACCTS. REC. COLLECTED	AMOUNT OF SALE	SALES TAX	CASH RECEIVED
	CASH SALES		994.00	59.64	1053.64
	BANK CREDIT CARD SALES		1290.00	77.40	1367.40
5081	KIM LEE	510.20			510.20
	TOTALS	510.20	2284.00	137.04	2931.24

CHARGE ACCOUNT SALES

CUSTOMER NO.	CUSTOMER NAME	AMOUNT OF SALE	SALES TAX	TOTAL RECEIVABLE
	TOTALS			

CASH REGISTER SUMMARY

06/11/X5

CASH COLLECTIONS

CUSTOMER NO.	SOURCE	ACCTS. REC. COLLECTED	AMOUNT OF SALE	SALES TAX	CASH RECEIVED
	CASH SALES		1060.00	63.60	1123.60
	BANK CREDIT CARD SALES				
1089	JEAN ALVAREZ	1000.00			1000.00
	TOTALS	1000.00	1060.00	63.60	2123.60

CHARGE ACCOUNT SALES

CUSTOMER NO.	CUSTOMER NAME	AMOUNT OF SALE	SALES TAX	TOTAL RECEIVABLE
7805	IRENE VIOLA	640.00	38.40	678.40
9672	ARNOLD WEXLER	3416.00	204.96	3620.96
	TOTALS	4056.00	243.36	4299.36

CASH REGISTER SUMMARY

CASH COLLECTIONS

CUSTOMER NO.	SOURCE	ACCTS. REC. COLLECTED	AMOUNT OF SALE	SALES TAX	CASH RECEIVED
	CASH SALES		1784.00	107.04	1891.04
	BANK CREDIT CARD SALES				
6770	GEORGE SACHS	116.60			116.60
	TOTALS	116.60	1784.00	107.04	2007.64

CHARGE ACCOUNT SALES

CUSTOMER NO.	CUSTOMER NAME	AMOUNT OF SALE	SALES TAX	TOTAL RECEIVABLE
6443	EDITH ROSS	48.00	2.88	50.88
	TOTALS	48.00	2.88	50.88

CASH REGISTER SUMMARY

CASH COLLECTIONS

CUSTOMER NO.	SOURCE	ACCTS. REC. COLLECTED	AMOUNT OF SALE	SALES TAX	CASH RECEIVED
	CASH SALES		342.00	20.52	362.52
	BANK CREDIT CARD SALES		3729.00	223.74	3952.74
	TOTALS		4071.00	244.26	4315.26

CHARGE ACCOUNT SALES

CUSTOMER NO.	CUSTOMER NAME	AMOUNT OF SALE	SALES TAX	TOTAL RECEIVABLE
9623	ABBY WASHINGTON	570.00	34.20	604.20
	TOTALS	570.00	34.20	604.20

CASH REGISTER SUMMARY

CASH COLLECTIONS

CUSTOMER NO.	SOURCE	ACCTS. REC. COLLECTED	AMOUNT OF SALE	SALES TAX	CASH RECEIVED
	CASH SALES		1677.00	100.62	1777.62
	BANK CREDIT CARD SALES				
4316	SYLVIA GERBER	341.67			341.67
	TOTALS	341.67	1677.00	100.62	2119.29

CHARGE ACCOUNT SALES

CUSTOMER NO.	CUSTOMER NAME	AMOUNT OF SALE	SALES TAX	TOTAL RECEIVABLE
3118	JAMES DOLAN	164.00	9.84	173.84
	TOTALS	164.00	9.84	173.84

CASH REGISTER SUMMARY

CASH COLLECTIONS

CUSTOMER NO.	SOURCE	ACCTS. REC. COLLECTED	AMOUNT OF SALE	SALES TAX	CASH RECEIVED
	CASH SALES		888.00	53.28	941.28
	BANK CREDIT CARD SALES				
	TOTALS		888.00	53.28	941.28

CHARGE ACCOUNT SALES

CUSTOMER NO.	CUSTOMER NAME	AMOUNT OF SALE	SALES TAX	TOTAL RECEIVABLE
	TOTALS			

CASH REGISTER SUMMARY

CASH COLLECTIONS

CUSTOMER NO.	SOURCE	ACCTS. REC. COLLECTED	AMOUNT OF SALE	SALES TAX	CASH RECEIVED
	CASH SALES		1240.00	74.40	1314.40
	BANK CREDIT CARD SALES		547.00	32.82	579.82
7805	IRENE VIOLA	140.70			140.70
	TOTALS	140.70	1787.00	107.22	2034.92

CHARGE ACCOUNT SALES

CUSTOMER NO.	CUSTOMER NAME	AMOUNT OF SALE	SALES TAX	TOTAL RECEIVABLE
7649	CAROL THOMPSON	1910.00	114.60	2024.60
	TOTALS	1910.00	114.60	2024.60

CASH REGISTER SUMMARY

CASH COLLECTIONS

CUSTOMER NO.	SOURCE	ACCTS. REC. COLLECTED	AMOUNT OF SALE	SALES TAX	CASH RECEIVED
	CASH SALES		1214.00	72.84	1286.84
	BANK CREDIT CARD SALES				
	TOTALS		1214.00	72.84	1286.84

CHARGE ACCOUNT SALES

CUSTOMER NO.	CUSTOMER NAME	AMOUNT OF SALE	SALES TAX	TOTAL RECEIVABLE
6281	MIRIAM RIGROSKI	166.00	9.96	175.96
	TOTALS	166.00	9.96	175.96

CASH REGISTER SUMMARY

06/19/X5

CASH COLLECTIONS

CUSTOMER NO.	SOURCE	ACCTS. REC. COLLECTED	AMOUNT OF SALE	SALES TAX	CASH RECEIVED
	CASH SALES		1506.00	90.36	1596.36
	BANK CREDIT CARD SALES		231.00	13.86	244.86
	TOTALS		1737.00	104.22	1841.22

CHARGE ACCOUNT SALES

CUSTOMER NO.	CUSTOMER NAME	AMOUNT OF SALE	SALES TAX	TOTAL RECEIVABLE
2369	FREIDA BERKLEY	120.00	7.20	127.20
	TOTALS	120.00	7.20	127.20

CASH REGISTER SUMMARY

06/20/X5

CASH COLLECTIONS

CUSTOMER NO.	SOURCE	ACCTS. REC. COLLECTED	AMOUNT OF SALE	SALES TAX	CASH RECEIVED
	CASH SALES		683.00	40.98	723.98
	BANK CREDIT CARD SALES		1158.00	69.48	1227.48
	TOTALS		1841.00	110.46	1951.46

CHARGE ACCOUNT SALES

CUSTOMER NO.	CUSTOMER NAME	AMOUNT OF SALE	SALES TAX	TOTAL RECEIVABLE
4277	WILLIAM HUBBARD	42.00	2.52	44.52
	TOTALS	42.00	2.52	44.52

CASH REGISTER SUMMARY

CASH COLLECTIONS

CUSTOMER NO.	SOURCE	ACCTS. REC. COLLECTED	AMOUNT OF SALE	SALES TAX	CASH RECEIVED
	CASH SALES		857.00	51.42	908.42
	BANK CREDIT CARD SALES		892.00	53.52	945.52
5748	JUAN QUINONES	72.93			72.93
	TOTALS	72.93	1749.00	104.94	1926.87

CHARGE ACCOUNT SALES

CUSTOMER NO.	CUSTOMER NAME	AMOUNT OF SALE	SALES TAX	TOTAL RECEIVABLE
6443	EDITH ROSS	2617.00	157.02	2774.02
	TOTALS	2617.00	157.02	2774.02

CASH REGISTER SUMMARY

CASH COLLECTIONS

CUSTOMER NO.	SOURCE	ACCTS. REC. COLLECTED	AMOUNT OF SALE	SALES TAX	CASH RECEIVED
	CASH SALES		1304.00	78.24	1382.24
	BANK CREDIT CARD SALES		480.00	28.80	508.80
3118	JAMES DOLAN	121.47			121.47
	TOTALS	121.47	1784.00	107.04	2012.51

CHARGE ACCOUNT SALES

CUSTOMER NO.	CUSTOMER NAME	AMOUNT OF SALE	SALES TAX	TOTAL RECEIVABLE
5081	KIM LEE	92.00	5.52	97.52
9864	HENRY ZACCARELLI	208.00	12.48	220.48
	TOTALS	300.00	18.00	318.00

CASH REGISTER SUMMARY

06/24/X5

CASH COLLECTIONS

CUSTOMER NO.	SOURCE	ACCTS. REC. COLLECTED	AMOUNT OF SALE	SALES TAX	CASH RECEIVED
	CASH SALES		1352.00	81.12	1433.12
	BANK CREDIT CARD SALES				
9672	ARNOLD WEXLER	3620.96			3620.96
	TOTALS	3620.96	1352.00	81.12	5054.08

CHARGE ACCOUNT SALES

CUSTOMER NO.	CUSTOMER NAME	AMOUNT OF SALE	SALES TAX	TOTAL RECEIVABLE
2745	MAX BUKOWSKI	1447.00	86.82	1533.82
	TOTALS	1447.00	86.82	1533.82

CASH REGISTER SUMMARY

06/25/X5

CASH COLLECTIONS

CUSTOMER NO.	SOURCE	ACCTS. REC. COLLECTED	AMOUNT OF SALE	SALES TAX	CASH RECEIVED
	CASH SALES		1731.00	103.86	1834.86
	BANK CREDIT CARD SALES				
2984	ROSE DELANEY	757.90			757.90
6907	STEPHEN SIDORSKY	744.12			744.12
	TOTALS	1502.02	1731.00	103.86	3336.88

CHARGE ACCOUNT SALES

CUSTOMER NO.	CUSTOMER NAME	AMOUNT OF SALE	SALES TAX	TOTAL RECEIVABLE
4316	SYLVIA GERBER	575.00	34.50	609.50
	TOTALS	575.00	34.50	609.50

CASH REGISTER SUMMARY

06/26/X5

CASH COLLECTIONS

CUSTOMER NO.	SOURCE	ACCTS. REC. COLLECTED	AMOUNT OF SALE	SALES TAX	CASH RECEIVED
	CASH SALES		1609.00	96.54	1705.54
	BANK CREDIT CARD SALES				
	TOTALS		1609.00	96.54	1705.54

CHARGE ACCOUNT SALES

CUSTOMER NO.	CUSTOMER NAME	AMOUNT OF SALE	SALES TAX	TOTAL RECEIVABLE
7805	IRENE VIOLA	376.00	22.56	398.56
	TOTALS	376.00	22.56	398.56

CASH REGISTER SUMMARY

06/27/X5

CASH COLLECTIONS

CUSTOMER NO.	SOURCE	ACCTS. REC. COLLECTED	AMOUNT OF SALE	SALES TAX	CASH RECEIVED
	CASH SALES		497.00	29.82	526.82
	BANK CREDIT CARD SALES		918.00	55.08	973.08
	TOTALS		1415.00	84.90	1499.90

CHARGE ACCOUNT SALES

CUSTOMER NO.	CUSTOMER NAME	AMOUNT OF SALE	SALES TAX	TOTAL RECEIVABLE
	TOTALS			

CASH REGISTER SUMMARY

06/29/X5

CASH COLLECTIONS

CUSTOMER NO.	SOURCE	ACCTS. REC. COLLECTED	AMOUNT OF SALE	SALES TAX	CASH RECEIVED
	CASH SALES		891.00	53.46	944.46
	BANK CREDIT CARD SALES		717.00	43.02	760.02
	TOTALS		1608.00	96.48	1704.48

CHARGE ACCOUNT SALES

CUSTOMER NO.	CUSTOMER NAME	AMOUNT OF SALE	SALES TAX	TOTAL RECEIVABLE
	TOTALS			

CASH REGISTER SUMMARY

06/30/X5

CASH COLLECTIONS

CUSTOMER NO.	SOURCE	ACCTS. REC. COLLECTED	AMOUNT OF SALE	SALES TAX	CASH RECEIVED
	CASH SALES		1961.00	117.66	2078.66
	BANK CREDIT CARD SALES				
6846	JOHN SCHUETZ	1000.00			1000.00
	TOTALS	1000.00	1961.00	117.66	3078.66

CHARGE ACCOUNT SALES

CUSTOMER NO.	CUSTOMER NAME	AMOUNT OF SALE	SALES TAX	TOTAL RECEIVABLE
9672	ARNOLD WEXLER	1159.00	69.54	1228.54
	TOTALS	1159.00	69.54	1228.54

CHECKBOOK AND
BANK RECONCILIATION

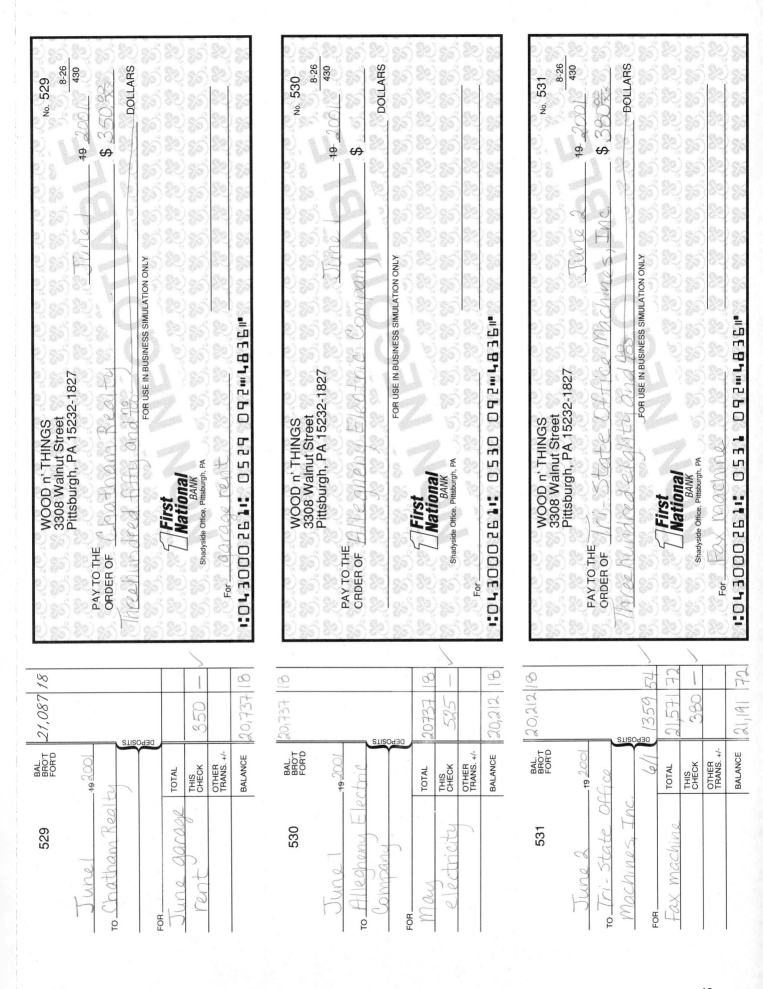

Check No. 529

WOOD n' THINGS
3308 Walnut Street
Pittsburgh, PA 15232-1827

No. 529   8-26/430

June 1, 19 2001

PAY TO THE ORDER OF Chatham Realty $ 350.00

Three hundred fifty and no/100 — DOLLARS

First National BANK
Shadyside Office, Pittsburgh, PA

FOR USE IN BUSINESS SIMULATION ONLY
NON-NEGOTIABLE

For garage rent

⑈043000261⑈ 0529 092 ⑈4836⑈

529		
BAL. BRO'T FOR'D		21,087 18
June 1, 19 2001		
TO Chatham Realty		
FOR June garage rent		
TOTAL		
THIS CHECK	350 —	
OTHER TRANS. +/-		
BALANCE		20,737 18

Check No. 530

WOOD n' THINGS
3308 Walnut Street
Pittsburgh, PA 15232-1827

No. 530   8-26/430

June 1, 19 2001

PAY TO THE ORDER OF Allegheny Electric Company $

— DOLLARS

First National BANK
Shadyside Office, Pittsburgh, PA

FOR USE IN BUSINESS SIMULATION ONLY
NON-NEGOTIABLE

For

⑈043000261⑈ 0530 092 ⑈4836⑈

530		
BAL. BRO'T FOR'D		20,737 18
June 1, 19 2001		
TO Allegheny Electric Company		
FOR May electricity		
TOTAL		20737 18
THIS CHECK	525 —	
OTHER TRANS. +/-		
BALANCE		20,212 18

Check No. 531

WOOD n' THINGS
3308 Walnut Street
Pittsburgh, PA 15232-1827

No. 531   8-26/430

June 2, 19 2001

PAY TO THE ORDER OF Tri-State Office Machines, Inc. $ 380.00

Three hundred eighty and 00/100 — DOLLARS

First National BANK
Shadyside Office, Pittsburgh, PA

FOR USE IN BUSINESS SIMULATION ONLY
NON-NEGOTIABLE

For Fax machine

⑈043000261⑈ 0531 092 ⑈4836⑈

531		
BAL. BRO'T FOR'D		20,212 18
June 2, 19 2001		
TO Tri-State Office Machines, Inc.		
FOR Fax machine		
6/1		1359 54
TOTAL		21,571 72
THIS CHECK	380 —	
OTHER TRANS. +/-		
BALANCE		21,191 72

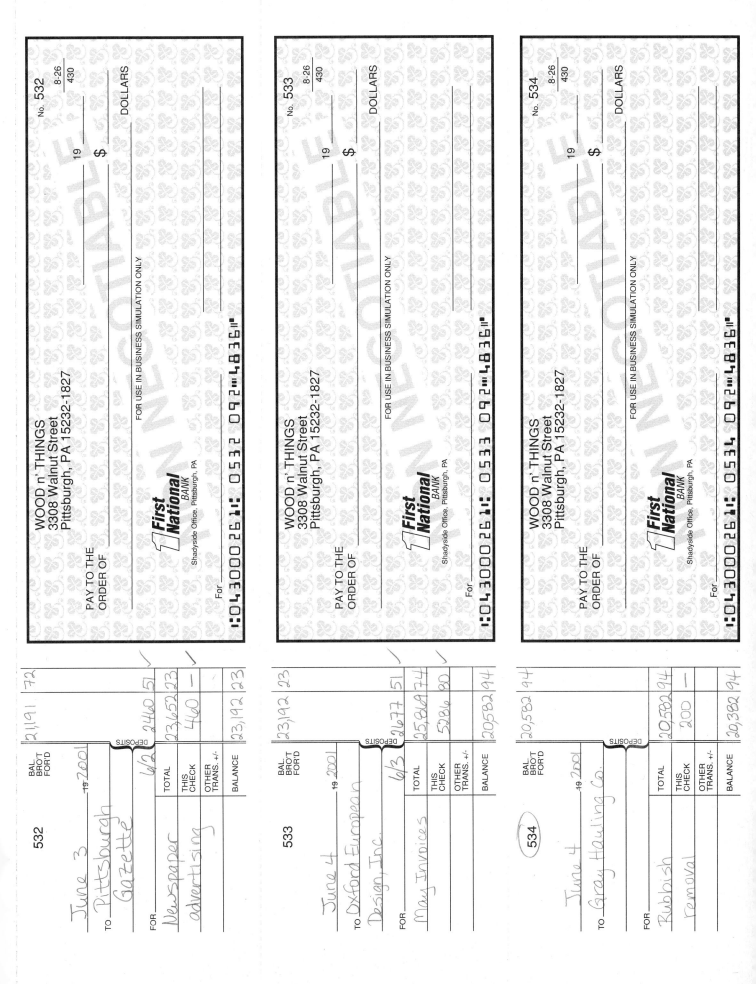

Check Register Stubs

	No. 535	No. 536	No. 537
Date	June 5, 19 2001	June 5, 19 2001	June 5, 19 2001
TO	First National Bank	Carnegie Shelving Company	Highland Insurance Agency
FOR	May employee withholdings & employer's taxes	May invoice less 2% discount	1-year fire insurance policy
BAL. BRO'T FORD	20,382 94	20,667 66	19,412 28
DEPOSITS	6/4 3344 72		
TOTAL	23,727 66	20,667 66	19,412 28
THIS CHECK	3060 —	1255 38	825 —
OTHER TRANS. +/-			
BALANCE	20,667 66	19,412 28	18,587 28

Checks

WOOD n' THINGS
3308 Walnut Street
Pittsburgh, PA 15232-1827

No. 535   8-26/430
19 ____ $ ____
PAY TO THE ORDER OF ____
____ DOLLARS

First National BANK
Shadyside Office, Pittsburgh, PA
For ____

⑆043000261⑆ 0535 092⑈4836⑈

WOOD n' THINGS
3308 Walnut Street
Pittsburgh, PA 15232-1827

No. 536   8-26/430
19 ____ $ ____
PAY TO THE ORDER OF ____
____ DOLLARS

First National BANK
Shadyside Office, Pittsburgh, PA
For ____

⑆043000261⑆ 0536 092⑈4836⑈

WOOD n' THINGS
3308 Walnut Street
Pittsburgh, PA 15232-1827

No. 537   8-26/430
19 ____ $ ____
PAY TO THE ORDER OF ____
____ DOLLARS

First National BANK
Shadyside Office, Pittsburgh, PA
For ____

⑆043000261⑆ 0537 092⑈4836⑈

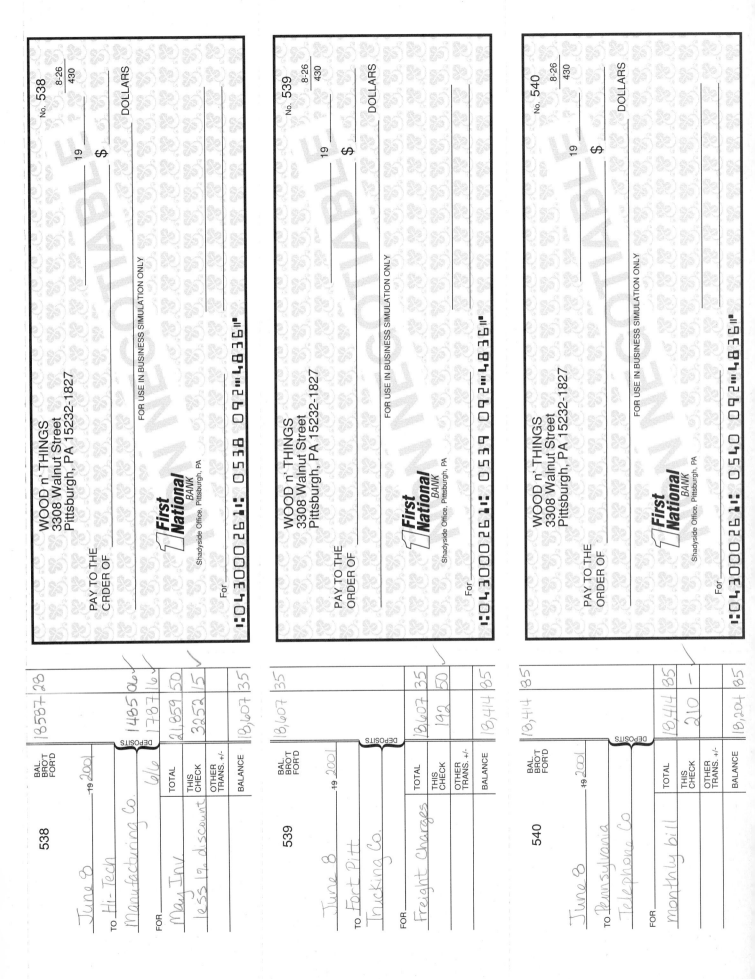

538

June 8 — 19 2001

TO Hi-Tech Manufacturing Co.

FOR May Inv
less 1% discount

BAL. BROT FOR'D	18,587 28
DEPOSITS	1,485 00 ✓
	1,787 16 ✓
TOTAL	21,859 50
THIS CHECK	3,252 15 ✓
OTHER TRANS. +/-	
BALANCE	18,607 35

539

June 8 — 19 2001

TO Fort Pitt Trucking Co.

FOR Freight Charges

BAL. BROT FOR'D	18,607 35
DEPOSITS	✓
TOTAL	18,607 35
THIS CHECK	192 50
OTHER TRANS. +/-	
BALANCE	18,414 85

540

June 8 — 19 2001

TO Pennsylvania Telephone Co

FOR monthly bill

BAL. BROT FOR'D	18,414 85
DEPOSITS	
TOTAL	18,414 85
THIS CHECK	210 —
OTHER TRANS. +/-	
BALANCE	18,204 85

WOOD n' THINGS
3308 Walnut Street
Pittsburgh, PA 15232-1827

No. 538
8-26
430

PAY TO THE ORDER OF _____

19 ___

$ _____

_____ DOLLARS

FOR USE IN BUSINESS SIMULATION ONLY

1 First National BANK
Shadyside Office, Pittsburgh, PA

For _____

⑈043000261⑈ 0538 092⑈4836⑈

WOOD n' THINGS
3308 Walnut Street
Pittsburgh, PA 15232-1827

No. 539
8-26
430

PAY TO THE ORDER OF _____

19 ___

$ _____

_____ DOLLARS

FOR USE IN BUSINESS SIMULATION ONLY

1 First National BANK
Shadyside Office, Pittsburgh, PA

For _____

⑈043000261⑈ 0539 092⑈4836⑈

WOOD n' THINGS
3308 Walnut Street
Pittsburgh, PA 15232-1827

No. 540
8-26
430

PAY TO THE ORDER OF _____

19 ___

$ _____

_____ DOLLARS

FOR USE IN BUSINESS SIMULATION ONLY

1 First National BANK
Shadyside Office, Pittsburgh, PA

For _____

⑈043000261⑈ 0540 092⑈4836⑈

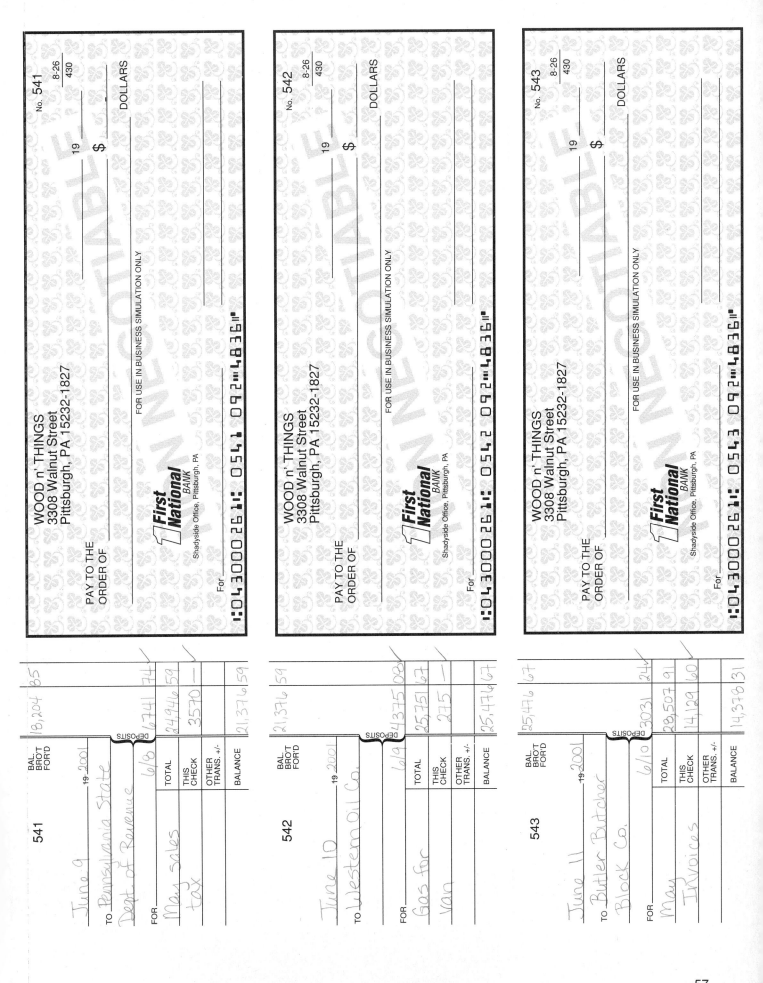

Check No. 541

WOOD n' THINGS
3308 Walnut Street
Pittsburgh, PA 15232-1827

No. 541
8-26 / 430

19 ____ $ ____

PAY TO THE ORDER OF ____

____ DOLLARS

First National BANK
Shadyside Office, Pittsburgh, PA

FOR USE IN BUSINESS SIMULATION ONLY

For ____

⑆043000261⑆ 0541 092 ⑈4836⑈

Check No. 542

WOOD n' THINGS
3308 Walnut Street
Pittsburgh, PA 15232-1827

No. 542
8-26 / 430

19 ____ $ ____

PAY TO THE ORDER OF ____

____ DOLLARS

First National BANK
Shadyside Office, Pittsburgh, PA

FOR USE IN BUSINESS SIMULATION ONLY

For ____

⑆043000261⑆ 0542 092 ⑈4836⑈

Check No. 543

WOOD n' THINGS
3308 Walnut Street
Pittsburgh, PA 15232-1827

No. 543
8-26 / 430

19 ____ $ ____

PAY TO THE ORDER OF ____

____ DOLLARS

First National BANK
Shadyside Office, Pittsburgh, PA

FOR USE IN BUSINESS SIMULATION ONLY

For ____

⑆043000261⑆ 0543 092 ⑈4836⑈

Register Stub 541

June 9, 19 2001
To Pennsylvania State Dept. of Revenue
FOR May Sales tax

BAL. BRO'T FOR'D	18,204 85
DEPOSITS 6/8	6741 74
TOTAL	24,946 59
THIS CHECK	3570 —
OTHER TRANS. +/-	
BALANCE	21,376 59

Register Stub 542

June 10, 19 2001
To Western Oil Co.
FOR Gas for Van

BAL. BRO'T FOR'D	21,376 59
DEPOSITS 6/9	4375 08
TOTAL	25,751 67
THIS CHECK	275 —
OTHER TRANS. +/-	
BALANCE	25,476 67

Register Stub 543

June 11, 19 2001
To Butler Butcher Block Co.
FOR May Invoices

BAL. BRO'T FOR'D	25,476 67
DEPOSITS 6/10	3031 24
TOTAL	28,507 91
THIS CHECK	14,129 60
OTHER TRANS. +/-	
BALANCE	14,378 31

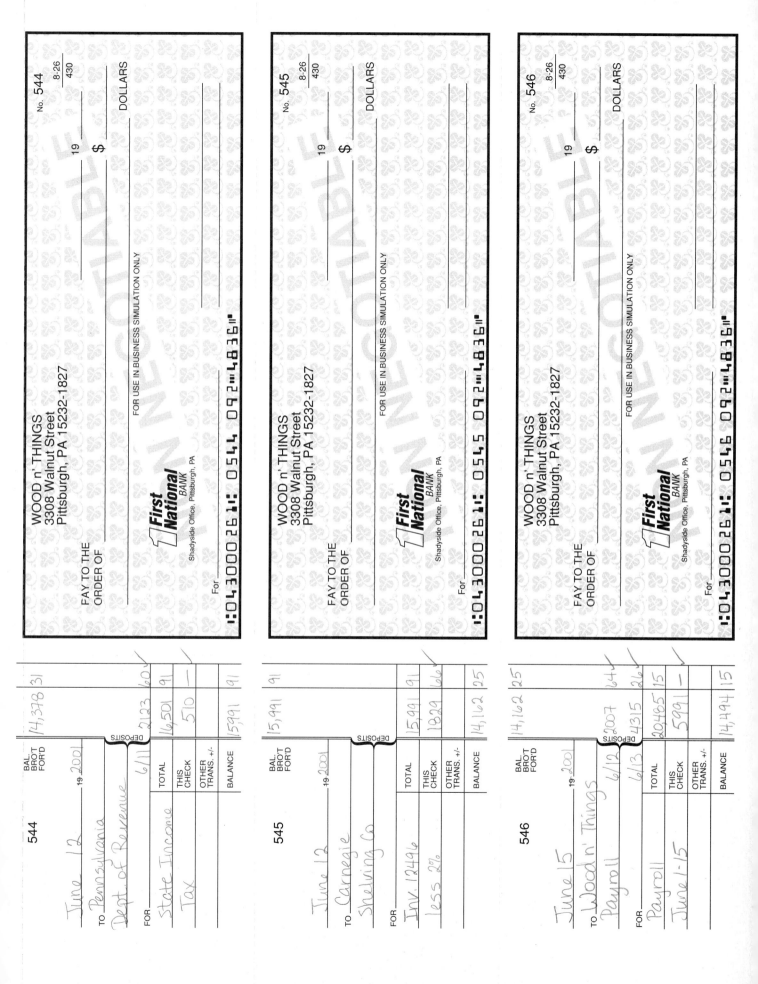

WOOD n' THINGS
3308 Walnut Street
Pittsburgh, PA 15232-1827

No. 544
8-26 / 430

19 ___ $ _____

PAY TO THE ORDER OF _____

_____ DOLLARS

First National BANK
Shadyside Office, Pittsburgh, PA

For _____

⑇0430002611⑇ 0544 092⑈4836⑈

WOOD n' THINGS
3308 Walnut Street
Pittsburgh, PA 15232-1827

No. 545
8-26 / 430

19 ___ $ _____

PAY TO THE ORDER OF _____

_____ DOLLARS

First National BANK
Shadyside Office, Pittsburgh, PA

For _____

⑇0430002611⑇ 0545 092⑈4836⑈

WOOD n' THINGS
3308 Walnut Street
Pittsburgh, PA 15232-1827

No. 546
8-26 / 430

19 ___ $ _____

PAY TO THE ORDER OF _____

_____ DOLLARS

First National BANK
Shadyside Office, Pittsburgh, PA

For _____

⑇0430002611⑇ 0546 092⑈4836⑈

544

BAL. BROT FORD	14,378	31

June 12, 19 2001
TO Pennsylvania Dept. of Revenue
FOR State Income Tax

DEPOSITS	6/11	2123	60
TOTAL		16,501	91
THIS CHECK		510	—
OTHER TRANS. +/-			
BALANCE		15,991	91

545

BAL. BROT FORD	15,991	91

June 12, 19 2001
TO Carnegie Shelving Co
FOR Inv. 12496 less 2%

DEPOSITS			
TOTAL		15,991	91
THIS CHECK		1829	66
OTHER TRANS. +/-			
BALANCE		14,162	25

546

BAL. BROT FORD	14,162	25

June 15, 19 2001
TO Wood n' Things Payroll
FOR Payroll June 1-15

DEPOSITS	6/12	2007	44
	6/13	4315	26
TOTAL		20,485	15
THIS CHECK		5991	—
OTHER TRANS. +/-			
BALANCE		14,494	15

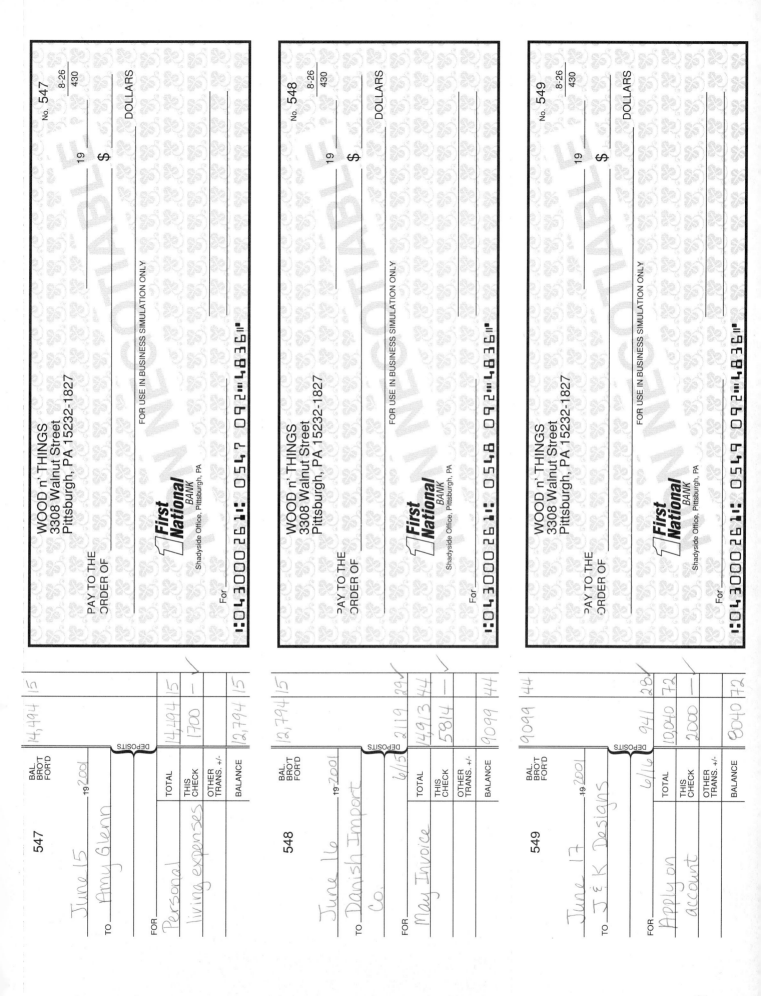

WOOD n' THINGS
3308 Walnut Street
Pittsburgh, PA 15232-1827

No. 547

8-26
430

19____

PAY TO THE
ORDER OF _____ $_____

_____ DOLLARS

First National BANK
Shadyside Office, Pittsburgh, PA

FOR USE IN BUSINESS SIMULATION ONLY

For _____

⑆043000261⑆ 0547 09⑈48 36⑈

WOOD n' THINGS
3308 Walnut Street
Pittsburgh, PA 15232-1827

No. 548

8-26
430

19____

PAY TO THE
ORDER OF _____ $_____

_____ DOLLARS

First National BANK
Shadyside Office, Pittsburgh, PA

FOR USE IN BUSINESS SIMULATION ONLY

For _____

⑆043000261⑆ 0548 09⑈48 36⑈

WOOD n' THINGS
3308 Walnut Street
Pittsburgh, PA 15232-1827

No. 549

8-26
430

19____

PAY TO THE
ORDER OF _____ $_____

_____ DOLLARS

First National BANK
Shadyside Office, Pittsburgh, PA

FOR USE IN BUSINESS SIMULATION ONLY

For _____

⑆043000261⑆ 0549 09⑈48 36⑈

547

June 15 19 2001
TO Amy Glenn

FOR Personal living expenses

	BAL. BRO'T FOR'D	14,494	15
DEPOSITS			
TOTAL	14,494	15
THIS CHECK	1700	—
OTHER TRANS. +/-		
BALANCE	12,794	15

548

June 16 19 2001
TO Danish Import Co.

FOR May Invoice

	BAL. BRO'T FOR'D	12,794	15
DEPOSITS	6/15	2119	29
TOTAL	14,913	44
THIS CHECK	5814	—
OTHER TRANS. +/-		
BALANCE	9099	44

549

June 17 19 2001
TO J&K Designs

FOR Apply on account

	BAL. BRO'T FOR'D	9099	44
DEPOSITS	6/16	941	28
TOTAL	10,040	72
THIS CHECK	2000	—
OTHER TRANS. +/-		
BALANCE	8040	72

61

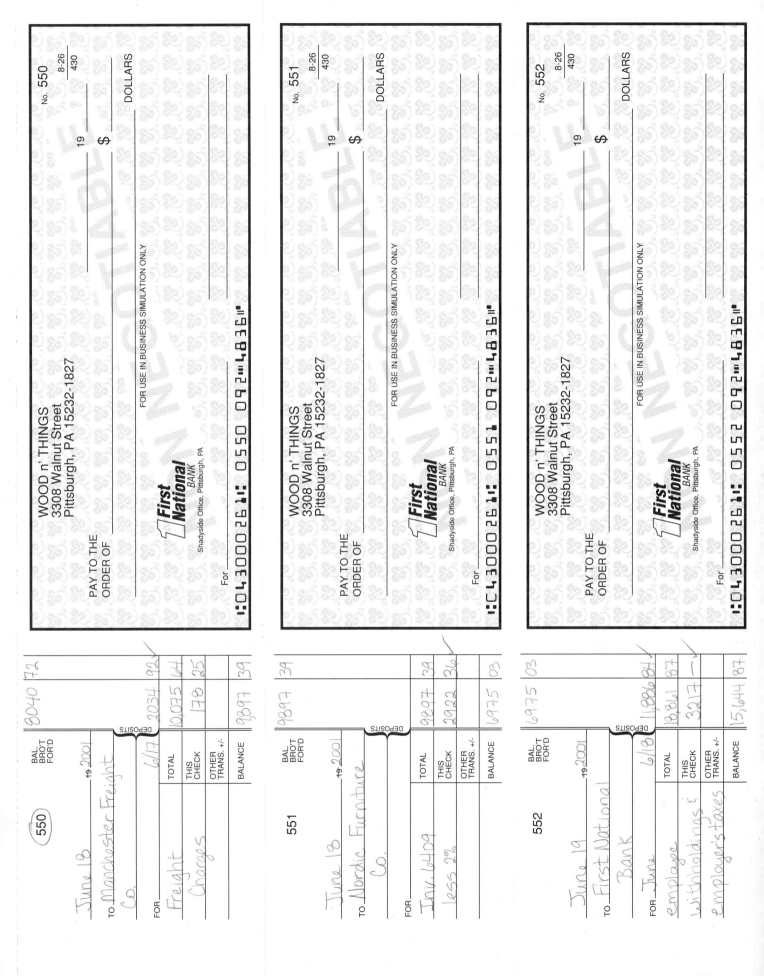

Check No. 550

WOOD n' THINGS
3308 Walnut Street
Pittsburgh, PA 15232-1827

No. 550

8-26 / 430

19___

PAY TO THE ORDER OF _____ $_____

_____ DOLLARS

First National BANK
Shadyside Office, Pittsburgh, PA

FOR USE IN BUSINESS SIMULATION ONLY

For _____

⑈043000261⑈ 0550 092⑈4836⑈

Check No. 551

WOOD n' THINGS
3308 Walnut Street
Pittsburgh, PA 15232-1827

No. 551

8-26 / 430

19___

PAY TO THE ORDER OF _____ $_____

_____ DOLLARS

First National BANK
Shadyside Office, Pittsburgh, PA

FOR USE IN BUSINESS SIMULATION ONLY

For _____

⑈043000261⑈ 0551 092⑈4836⑈

Check No. 552

WOOD n' THINGS
3308 Walnut Street
Pittsburgh, PA 15232-1827

No. 552

8-26 / 430

19___

PAY TO THE ORDER OF _____ $_____

_____ DOLLARS

First National BANK
Shadyside Office, Pittsburgh, PA

FOR USE IN BUSINESS SIMULATION ONLY

For _____

⑈043000261⑈ 0552 092⑈4836⑈

Check Stub 550

June 18, 2001
To Manchester Freight Co.
For Freight Charges

BAL. BROT FORD	8040	72
DEPOSITS 6/17	2034	00
TOTAL	10,075	64
THIS CHECK	178	25
OTHER TRANS. +/-		
BALANCE	9897	39

Check Stub 551

June 18, 2001
To Nordic Furniture Co.
For Inv. 6409 less 2%

BAL. BROT FORD	9897	39
DEPOSITS		
TOTAL	9897	39
THIS CHECK	2922	36
OTHER TRANS. +/-		
BALANCE	6975	03

Check Stub 552

June 19, 2001
To First National Bank
For June employee withholdings & employer's taxes

BAL. BROT FORD	6975	03
DEPOSITS 6/18	11,886	84
TOTAL	18,861	87
THIS CHECK	3217	—
OTHER TRANS. +/-		
BALANCE	15,644	87

WOOD n' THINGS
3308 Walnut Street
Pittsburgh, PA 15232-1827

No. 553
8-26
430

PAY TO THE
ORDER OF _____ $ _____
_____ DOLLARS
19 ___

First National BANK
Shadyside Office, Pittsburgh, PA

FOR USE IN BUSINESS SIMULATION ONLY

For _____

⑆043000261⑆ 0553 092⑈4836⑈

WOOD n' THINGS
3308 Walnut Street
Pittsburgh, PA 15232-1827

No. 554
8-26
430

PAY TO THE
ORDER OF _____ $ _____
_____ DOLLARS
19 ___

First National BANK
Shadyside Office, Pittsburgh, PA

FOR USE IN BUSINESS SIMULATION ONLY

For _____

⑆043000261⑆ 0554 092⑈4836⑈

WOOD n' THINGS
3308 Walnut Street
Pittsburgh, PA 15232-1827

No. 555
8-26
430

PAY TO THE
ORDER OF _____ $ _____
_____ DOLLARS
19 ___

First National BANK
Shadyside Office, Pittsburgh, PA

FOR USE IN BUSINESS SIMULATION ONLY

For _____

⑆043000261⑆ 0555 092⑈4836⑈

553

June 19, 19 2001
TO Monroe Savings &
Loan Assoc.
FOR Mortgage &
Interest

BAL. BRO'T FOR'D	15,044	87
DEPOSITS		
TOTAL	15,044	87
THIS CHECK	1500	—
OTHER TRANS. +/-		
BALANCE	14,084	87

554

June 22, 19 2001
TO Danish Import
Co.
FOR Invoice 8964

BAL. BRO'T FOR'D	14,084	87
DEPOSITS	6/19 1841	22
	6/20 1451	46
TOTAL	17,877	55
THIS CHECK	3833	—
OTHER TRANS. +/-		
BALANCE	14,044	55

555

June 23, 19 2001
TO Oxford European
Design, Inc.
FOR Invoice #6098
less Credit
Memo 211

BAL. BRO'T FOR'D	14,044	55
DEPOSITS	6/22 1926	87
TOTAL	15,971	42
THIS CHECK	890	—
OTHER TRANS. +/-		
BALANCE	15,081	42

Check No. 556

WOOD n' THINGS
3308 Walnut Street
Pittsburgh, PA 15232-1827

No. 556

8-26 / 430

19___ $___

PAY TO THE ORDER OF _____ DOLLARS

First National BANK
Shadyside Office, Pittsburgh, PA

For _____

⑆0430002611⑆ 0556 092 ⑈4836⑈

Stub 556

556		
June 24 19 200_	BAL. BROT FORD	15,081 42
TO Nordic Furniture Co.	DEPOSITS	
	6/23 2012 51	
FOR Invoice 9920 less Credit Memo 1863 – 2%	TOTAL	17,093 93
	THIS CHECK	1735 58
	OTHER TRANS. +/-	
	BALANCE	15,358 35

Check No. 557

WOOD n' THINGS
3308 Walnut Street
Pittsburgh, PA 15232-1827

No. 557

8-26 / 430

19___ $___

PAY TO THE ORDER OF _____ DOLLARS

First National BANK
Shadyside Office, Pittsburgh, PA

For _____

⑆0430002611⑆ 0557 092 ⑈4836⑈

Stub 557

557		
June 25 19 200_	BAL. BROT FORD	15,358 35
TO William Sloan	DEPOSITS	
	6/24 5054 08	
FOR Legal Fee	TOTAL	20,412 43
	THIS CHECK	110
	OTHER TRANS. +/-	1 –
	BALANCE	20,302 43

Check No. 558

WOOD n' THINGS
3308 Walnut Street
Pittsburgh, PA 15232-1827

No. 558

8-26 / 430

19___ $___

PAY TO THE ORDER OF _____ DOLLARS

First National BANK
Shadyside Office, Pittsburgh, PA

For _____

⑆0430002611⑆ 0558 092 ⑈4836⑈

Stub 558

558		
June 26 19 200_	BAL. BROT FORD	20,302 43
TO Western Oil Co.	DEPOSITS	
	6/25 3336 88	
FOR Gas for Delivery Van	TOTAL	23,639 31
	THIS CHECK	92 –
	OTHER TRANS. +/-	
	BALANCE	23,547 31

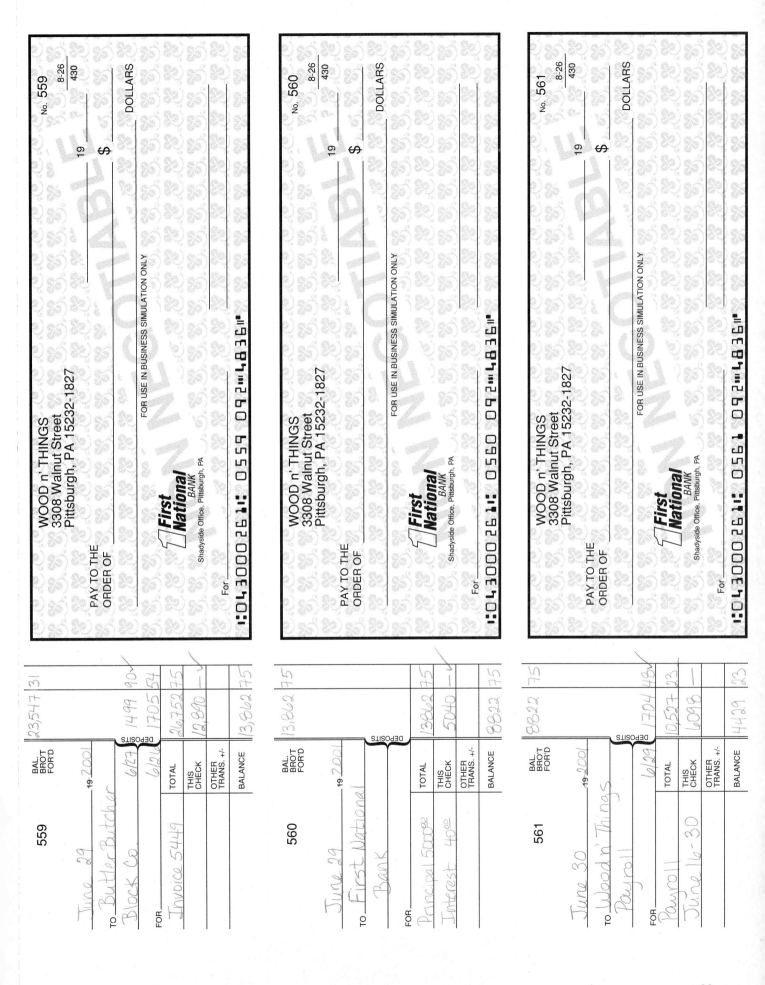

559

June 29 _____ 19 2001

TO Butler Butcher

Block Co.

FOR Invoice 5449

		DEPOSITS
BAL. BROT FORD	23,547	31
6/27	1499	90 ✓
6/28	1705	54
TOTAL	26,752	75
THIS CHECK	12,890	— ✓
OTHER TRANS. +/-		
BALANCE	13,862	75

560

June 29 _____ 19 2001

TO First National

Bank

FOR Principal 5000⁰⁰
Interest 40⁰⁰

		DEPOSITS
BAL. BROT FORD	13,862	75
TOTAL	13,862	75
THIS CHECK	5040	— ✓
OTHER TRANS. +/-		
BALANCE	8822	75

561

June 30 _____ 19 2001

TO Wood n' Things

Payroll

FOR Payroll
June 16-30

		DEPOSITS
BAL. BROT FORD	8822	75
6/29	1704	48 ✓
TOTAL	10,527	23
THIS CHECK	6098	—
OTHER TRANS. +/-		
BALANCE	4429	23

WOOD n' THINGS
3308 Walnut Street
Pittsburgh, PA 15232-1827

No. 559
8-26
430

19 _____

PAY TO THE
ORDER OF _____ $ _____

_____ DOLLARS

FOR USE IN BUSINESS SIMULATION ONLY

First National BANK
Shadyside Office, Pittsburgh, PA

For _____

⑈⑈430002611⑈⑈ 0559 092⑈⑈4836⑈⑈

WOOD n' THINGS
3308 Walnut Street
Pittsburgh, PA 15232-1827

No. 560
8-26
430

19 _____

PAY TO THE
ORDER OF _____ $ _____

_____ DOLLARS

FOR USE IN BUSINESS SIMULATION ONLY

First National BANK
Shadyside Office, Pittsburgh, PA

For _____

⑈⑈430002611⑈⑈ 0560 092⑈⑈4836⑈⑈

WOOD n' THINGS
3308 Walnut Street
Pittsburgh, PA 15232-1827

No. 561
8-26
430

19 _____

PAY TO THE
ORDER OF _____ $ _____

_____ DOLLARS

FOR USE IN BUSINESS SIMULATION ONLY

First National BANK
Shadyside Office, Pittsburgh, PA

For _____

⑈⑈430002611⑈⑈ 0561 092⑈⑈4836⑈⑈

WOOD n' THINGS
3308 Walnut Street
Pittsburgh, PA 15232-1827

No. 562

8-26
___
430

19___ $___

PAY TO THE
ORDER OF _____

_____ DOLLARS

First National BANK
Shadyside Office, Pittsburgh, PA

FOR USE IN BUSINESS SIMULATION ONLY

For _____

⑈043000261⑈ 0562 092⑈4836⑈

WOOD n' THINGS
3308 Walnut Street
Pittsburgh, PA 15232-1827

No. 563

8-26
___
430

19___ $___

PAY TO THE
ORDER OF _____

_____ DOLLARS

First National BANK
Shadyside Office, Pittsburgh, PA

FOR USE IN BUSINESS SIMULATION ONLY

For _____

⑈043000261⑈ 0563 092⑈4836⑈

WOOD n' THINGS
3308 Walnut Street
Pittsburgh, PA 15232-1827

No. 564

8-26
___
430

19___ $___

PAY TO THE
ORDER OF _____

_____ DOLLARS

First National BANK
Shadyside Office, Pittsburgh, PA

FOR USE IN BUSINESS SIMULATION ONLY

For _____

⑈043000261⑈ 0564 092⑈4836⑈

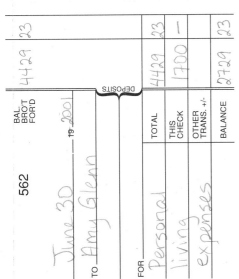

562

BAL. BROT FORD	4429	23
June 30 19 2001		
TO Amy Glenn		
FOR Personal living expenses		
DEPOSITS		
TOTAL	4429	23
THIS CHECK	1700	—
OTHER TRANS. +/-		
BALANCE	2729	23

563

BAL. BROT FORD	2729	23
June 30 19 2001		
TO Eleanor Chae		
FOR Reimburse Petty cash Service Charge		
DEPOSITS		
TOTAL	2729	23
THIS CHECK	46	1
OTHER TRANS. +/-	(173	31)
BALANCE	2509	92

564

BAL. BROT FORD	2509	92
19 2001		
TO		
FOR		
DEPOSITS 6/30	3078	66
TOTAL	5588	58
THIS CHECK		
OTHER TRANS. +/-		
BALANCE		

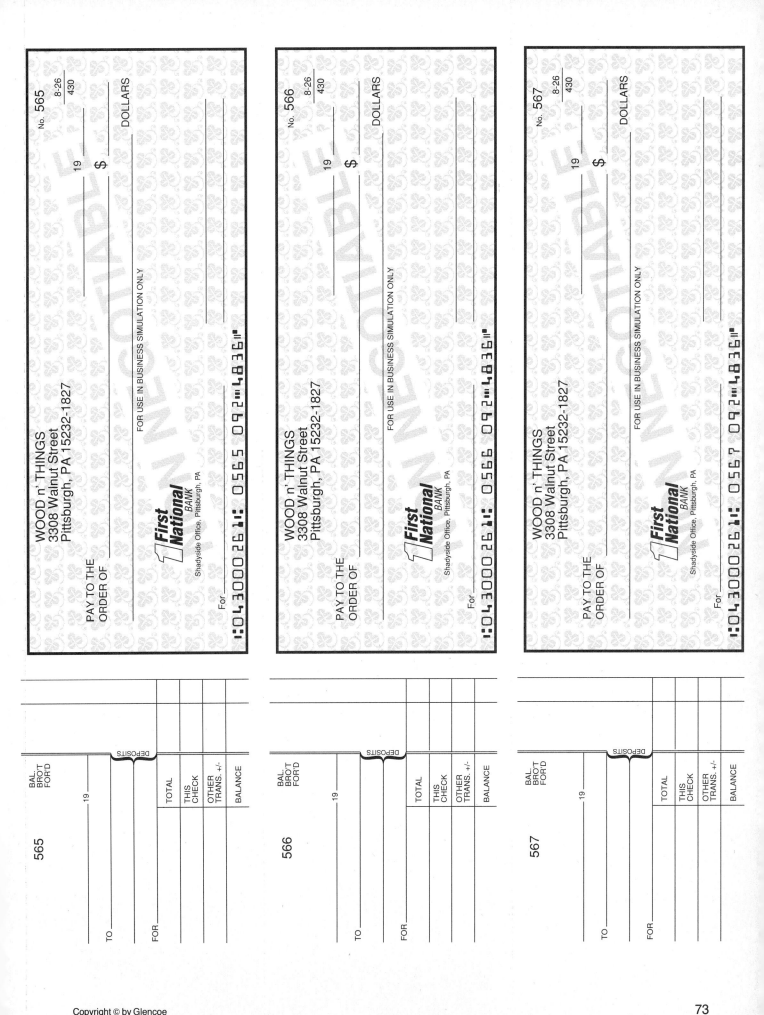

Wood n' Things

Bank Reconciliation

June 30, 19X5

Bank Statement				
Ending Balance				11622 17
Outstanding Deposit				3078 66
				14700 83
Outstanding Checks	534	200 —		
	550	178 25		
	555	890 —		
	561	6098 —		
	562	1700 —		
	563	46 —	9112 25	
			5588 58	
Checkbook				
Ending Balance				5761 89
Less Service Charge				173 31
			5588 58	

JOURNALS

SALES JOURNAL

PAGE 35

DATE 2001	CUST. NO.	CUSTOMER'S NAME	POST. REF.	ACCOUNTS RECEIVABLE DEBIT 111	SALES TAX PAYABLE CREDIT 231	SALES CREDIT 401
June 1	6770	George Sachs	✓	1 16 60	6 60	1 10 —
2	1089	Jean Alvarez	✓	9 28 56	52 56	8 76 —
3	2984	Rose Delaney	✓	7 57 90	42 90	7 15 —
5	3118	James Dolan	✓	59 36	3 36	56 —
5	6281	Miriam Rigroski	✓	4 24 —	24 —	4 00 —
				22 86 42	1 29 42	21 57 —
8	6770	George Sachs	✓	4 08 10	23 10	3 85 —
8	6907	Stephen Sidorsky	✓	2 43 80	13 80	2 30 —
9	4316	Sylvia Gerber	✓	59 36	3 36	56 —
11	7805	Irene Viola	✓	6 78 40	38 40	6 40 —
11	9672	Arnold Wexler	✓	36 20 96	2 04 96	34 16 —
12	6443	Edith Ross	✓	50 88	2 88	48 —
13	9623	Abby Washington	✓	6 04 20	34 20	5 70 —
				56 65 70	3 20 70	53 45 —
15	3118	James Dolan	✓	1 73 84	9 84	1 64 —
17	7649	Carol Thompson	✓	20 24 60	1 14 60	19 10 —
18	6281	Miriam Rigroski	✓	1 75 96	9 96	1 66 —
19	2369	Freida Berkley	✓	1 27 20	7 20	1 20 —
20	4277	William Hubbard	✓	44 52	2 52	42 —
				25 46 12	1 44 12	24 02 —
22	6443	Edith Ross	✓	27 74 02	1 57 02	26 17 —
23	5081	Kim Lee	✓	97 52	5 52	92 —
23	9864	Henry Zaccarelli	✓	2 20 48	12 48	2 08 —
24	2745	Max Bukowski	✓	15 33 82	86 82	14 47 —
25	4316	Sylvia Gerber	✓	6 09 50	34 50	5 75 —
26	7805	Irene Viola	✓	3 98 56	22 56	3 76 —
30	9672	Arnold Wexler	✓	12 28 54	69 54	11 59 —
				68 62 44	3 88 44	64 74 —
				1 73 60 68	9 82 68	1 63 78 —
				(111)	(231)	(401)

CASH RECEIPTS JOURNAL

DATE 2001	EXPLANATION	POST. REF.	ACCOUNTS RECEIVABLE CREDIT	SALES TAX PAYABLE CREDIT	SALES CREDIT	OTHER ACCOUNTS CREDIT			CASH DEBIT
						ACCOUNT TITLE	POST. REF.	AMOUNT	
June 1	Cash Sales			7260	1210 —				128260
1	Arnold Wexler	✓	76 94						76 94
2	Cash Sales			11760	1960 —				207760
2	Edith Ross	✓	38291						38291
3	Cash Sales			12870	2145 —				227370
3	Henry Zaccarelli	✓	40381						40381
4	Cash Sales			10548	1758 —				186348
4	Bank Credit Card Sales			2724	454 —				43124
4	John Schuetz	✓	1000 —						1000 —
5	Cash Sales			8406	1401 —				148506
6	Cash Sales			2880	480 —				50880
6	Bank Credit Card Sales			7236	1206 —				127836
			186366	63684	10614 —				1317450
8	Cash Sales			11172	1862 —				197372
8	William Hubbard	✓	500 —						500 —
8	Carol Thompson	✓	426802						426802
10	Highland Ins. Agency					Prepaid Ins.	131	100 —	100 —
9	Cash Sales			14148	2358 —				249948
9	Bank Credit Card Sales			5034	839 —				88934
9	Max Bukowski	✓	98626						98626
10	Cash Sales			5964	994 —				105364
10	Bank Credit Card Sales			7740	1290 —				136740
10	Kim Lee	✓	51020						51020
11	Cash Sales			6360	1060 —				112360
11	Jean Alvarez	✓	1000 —						1000 —
12	Cash Sales			10704	1784 —				189104
12	George Sachs	✓	11660						11660
13	Cash Sales			2052	342 —				36252
13	Bank Credit Card Sales			22374	3729 —				395274
			738108	85548	14258 —			100 —	2259456
15	Cash Sales			10062	1677 —				177762
15	Sylvia Gerber	✓	34167						34167
16	Cash Sales			5328	888 —				94128
17	Cash Sales			7440	1240 —				131440
17	Bank Credit Card Sales			3282	547 —				57982
17	Irene Viola	✓	14070						14070

DATE 2001	EXPLANATION	POST. REF.	ACCOUNTS RECEIVABLE CREDIT	SALES TAX PAYABLE CREDIT	SALES CREDIT	OTHER ACCOUNTS CREDIT ACCOUNT TITLE	POST. REF.	AMOUNT	CASH DEBIT
June 18	Matured CD					Short-Term Invest.	106	10000—	
						Interest Income	491	600—	10600—
18	Cash Sales			7284	1214—				128684
19	Cash Sales			9036	1506—				159636
19	Bank Credit Card Sales			1386	231—				24486
20	Cash Sales			4098	683—				72378
20	Bank Credit Card Sales			6948	1158—				122748
			48237	54864	9144—			10600—	2077501
22	Cash Sales			5142	857—				90842
22	Bank Credit Card Sales			5352	892—				94552
22	Juan Quinones	✓	7293						7293
23	Cash Sales			7824	1304—				138224
23	Bank Credit Card Sales			2880	480—				50880
23	James Dolan	✓	12147						12147
24	Cash Sales			8112	1352—				143312
24	Arnold Wexler	✓	362096						362096
25	Cash Sales			10386	1731—				183486
25	Rose Delaney	✓	75790						75790
25	Stephen Sidorsky	✓	74412						74412
26	Cash Sales			9654	1609—				170534
27	Cash Sales			2982	497—				52682
27	Bank Credit Card Sales			5508	918—				97308
29	Cash Sales			5346	891—				94446
29	Bank Credit Card Sales			4302	717—				76002
30	Cash Sales			11766	1961—				207866
	John Schuetz	✓	1000—						1000—
			631738	79254	13209—				2031892
			1104449	283350	47225—			10700—	7680299
			(111)	(231)	(401)			(X)	(101)

Copyright © by Glencoe

DATE 2001	CK. NO.	PAYEE	POST. REF.	ACCOUNTS PAYABLE DEBIT	OTHER ACCOUNTS DEBIT — ACCOUNT TITLE	POST. REF.	AMOUNT	PURCHASES DISCOUNT CREDIT	CASH CREDIT
June 1	529	Chatham Realty			Rent Exp.-Garage	611	350 —		350 —
1	530	Allegheny Electric Co.			Utilities Exp.	612	525 —		525 —
2	531	Tri-State Office Machine Inc			Store Fixtures & Equip.	145	380 —		380 —
3	532	Pittsburgh Gazette			Advertising Exp.	624	460 —		460 —
4	533	Oxford European Design, Inc	✓	528680					528680
4	534	Gray Hauling Co.			Rubbish Removal Exp.	625	200 —		200 —
5	535	First National Bank			Soc. Sec. Tax Pay.	221	553 —		3060 —
5					Medicare Tax Pay.	222	127 —		
5					Fed. Income Tax Pay.	223	1700 —		
5					Payroll Taxes Pay.	226	680 —		
5	536	Carnegie Shelving Co	✓	1281 —				2562	125538
5	537	Highland Insurance Co			Prepaid Insurance	131	825 —		825 —
				656780			5800 —	2562	1234218
8	538	Hi-Tech Manufacturing Co	✓	3285 —				3285	325215
8	539	Fort Pitt Trucking Co			Freight In	506	19250		19250
8	540	Pennsylvania Telephone Co.			Telephone Exp.	613	210 —		210 —
9	541	Penn. State Dept. of Revenue			Sales Tax Pay.	231	3570 —		3570 —
10	542	Western Oil Co.			Delivery Exp.	623	275 —		275 —
11	543	Butler Butcher Block Co	✓	1412960					1412960
12	544	Penn. Dept. of Revenue			State Income Tax Pay.	224	5110 —		5110 —
12	545	Carnegie Shelving Co.	✓	18867 —				3734	1829466
				1928160			475750	7019	2396891
15	546	Wood n' Things Payroll			Salaries Payable	205	5991 —		5991 —
15	547	Amy Glenn			Amy Glenn, Drawing	302	1700 —		1700 —
16	548	Danish Import Co.	✓	5814 —					5814 —
17	549	J & K Designs	✓	2000 —					2000 —
18	550	Manchester Freight Co.			Freight In	506	17825		17825
18	551	Nordic Furniture Co.	✓	2982 —				5964	292236
19	552	First National Bank			Soc. Sec. Tax Pay.	221	570 —		3217 —
19					Medicare Tax Pay.	222	131 —		
19					Fed. Income Tax Pay.	223	1815 —		
19					Payroll Taxes Pay.	226	701 —		
19	553	Monroe Savings & Loan Assoc.			Mortgage Pay.	251	600 —		1560 —
					Interest Exp.	691	960 —		
				10796 —			1264625	5964	2338261
22	554	Danish Import Co.	✓	3833 —					3833 —
23	555	Oxford European Design, Inc.	✓	890 —					890 —
24	556	Nordic Furniture Co.	✓	1771 —				3542	173558
25	557	William Sloan			Acct. & Legal Exp.	633	1110 —		1110 —
26	558	Western Oil Co			Delivery Exp.	623	92 —		92 —
29	559	Butler Butcher Block Co.	✓	12890 —					12890 —
29	560	First National Bank			Notes Payable	201	5000 —		5040 —
					Interest Exp.	691	40 —		

CASH PAYMENTS JOURNAL

DATE 2001	CK. NO.	PAYEE	POST. REF.	ACCOUNTS PAYABLE DEBIT	OTHER ACCOUNTS DEBIT			PURCHASES DISCOUNT CREDIT	CASH CREDIT
					ACCOUNT TITLE	POST. REF.	AMOUNT		
June 30	561	Wood n' Things Payroll			Salaries Pay.	205	6098 —		6098 —
30	562	Amy Glenn			Amy Glenn, Drawing	302	1700 —		1700 —
30	563	Eleanor Chae			Store Supplies	133	11 —		46 —
					Office Supplies	135	12 —		
					Delivery Exp.	623	23 —		
				19384 —			13086 —	3542	3243458
				5602940			3628975	19087	9212828
30	—	Noncheck			Discount Exp. on Bank Credit Card Sales	634	17331		17331
				5602940			3646306	19087	9230159
				(202)			(X)	(553)	(101)

DATE 2001	PURCHASED FROM	INVOICE NUMBER	INV. DATE	TERMS	POST. REF.	PURCHASES DR ACCOUNTS PAYABLE CR.
June 2	Butler Butcher Block Co.	5449	5/29	n/30	✓	12 8 9 0 —
3	Carnegie Shelving Co.	12496	6/2	2/10, n/30	✓	1 8 6 7 —
4	Danish Import Co.	8964	6/1	n/30	✓	3 8 3 3 —
						18 5 9 0 —
9	Oxford European Design, Inc.	6098	6/5	n/30	✓	1 4 1 7 —
9	Woodcraft, Inc.	809	6/8	n/30	✓	1 7 1 5 —
11	Nordic Furniture Co.	6409	6/9	2/10, n/30	✓	2 9 8 2 —
						6 1 1 4 —
16	Butler Butcher Block Co.	8902	6/11	n/30	✓	4 9 8 4 —
17	Nordic Furniture Co.	9920	6/15	2/10, n/30	✓	2 0 2 1 —
18	Danish Import Co.	9113	6/16	n/30	✓	3 5 2 9 —
						10 5 3 4 —
22	Nordic Furniture Co.	9987	6/19	2/10, n/30	✓	3 9 2 4 —
24	Carnegie Shelving Co.	20249	6/22	2/10, n/30	✓	1 4 8 3 —
26	Oxford European Design, Inc.	8821	6/23	n/30	✓	6 2 1 —
						6 0 2 8 —
						41 2 6 6 —
						(501) (202)

GENERAL JOURNAL

	DATE	DESCRIPTION	POST. REF.	DEBIT	CREDIT	
	2001					
1	June 11	Accounts Payable, Oxford European Design, Inc.	202 ✓	527 —		1
2		Purchases Returns & Allowances	551		527 —	2
3		Received Credit Memo 211 for Inv. #6093 dated				3
4		June 5 for damaged furniture				4
5						5
6	15	Sales Salaries Expense	601	6000 —		6
7		Office Salaries Expense	602	1540 —		7
8		Stockroom Salaries Expense	603	1230 —		8
9		Social Security Tax Payable	221		570 —	9
10		Medicare Tax Payable	222		131 —	10
11		Federal Income Tax Payable	223		1815 —	11
12		State Income Tax Payable	224		263 —	12
13		Salaries Payable	205		5991 —	13
14		Record total payroll June 1–15				14
15						15
16	15	Payroll Taxes Expense	607	701 —		16
17		Payroll Taxes Payable	226		701 —	17
18		Employer's portion Soc. Sec. $570 &				18
19		Medicare $131				19
20						20
21	17	Sales Returns & Allowances	441	20 —		21
22		Accounts Receivable, James Dolan	111 ✓		20 —	22
23		Issued Credit Memo 105 for damaged				23
24		merchandise				24
25						25
26	19	Accounts Payable, Nordic Furniture Co.	202 ✓	250 —		26
27		Purchases Returns & Allowances	551		250 —	27
28		Received Credit Memo 1863 dated June 15				28
29		for wrong colored chairs				29
30						30
31	22	Allowance for Uncollectible Accounts	112 ✓	112 87		31
32		Accounts Receivable, James Tashiko	111 ✓		112 87	32
33		Wrote off James Tashiko account				33
34		as uncollectible				34
35						35
36	26	Sales Returns & Allowances	441	97 52		36
37		Accounts Receivable, Kim Lee	111 ✓		97 52	37
38		Issued Credit Memo 106 for				38
39		merchandise return				39
40						40
41						41
42						42
43						43
44						44
45						45

	DATE	DESCRIPTION	POST. REF.	DEBIT	CREDIT	
	2001					
1	June 30	Sales Salaries Expense	601	6200 —		1
2		Office Salaries Expense	602	1480 —		2
3		Stockroom Salaries Expense	603	1230 —		3
4		Social Security Tax Payable	221		579 —	4
5		Medicare Tax Payable	222		133 —	5
6		Federal Income Tax Payable	223		1833 —	6
7		State Income Tax Payable	224		267 —	7
8		Salaries Payable	205		6098 —	8
9		Record total payroll June 16-30				9
10						10
11	30	Payroll Taxes Expense	607	712 —		11
12		Payroll Taxes Payable	226		712 —	12
13		Employer's portion Soc. Sec. $570 &				13
14		Medicare $131				14
15						15
16						16
17						17
18						18
19						19
20						20
21						21
22						22
23						23
24						24
25						25
26						26
27						27
28						28
29						29
30						30
31						31
32						32
33						33
34						34
35						35
36						36
37						37
38						38
39						39
40						40
41						41
42						42
43						43
44						44
45						45

GENERAL JOURNAL

	DATE		DESCRIPTION	POST. REF.	DEBIT	CREDIT	
1	2001		Adjusting Entries				1
2	June	30	Income Summary	399	67862		2
3	a		Merchandise Inventory	121		67862 —	3
4							4
5	b	30	Merchandise Inventory	121	62738 —		5
6			Income Summary	399		62738 —	6
7							7
8	c	30	Loss from Uncollectible Accounts	632	106849		8
9			Allowance for Uncollectible Accounts	112		106849	9
10							10
11	d	30	Interest Receivable	115	150 —		11
12			Interest Income	491		150 —	12
13							13
14	e	30	Insurance Expense	631	3145 —		14
15			Prepaid Insurance	131		3145 —	15
16							16
17	f	30	Store Supplies Expense	621	1741 —		17
18			Store Supplies	133		1741 —	18
19							19
20	g	30	Office Supplies Expense	622	642 —		20
21			Office Supplies	135		642 —	21
22							22
23	h	30	Depreciation Expense	641	17730 —		23
24			Accumulated Depreciation-Building	144		12000 —	24
25			Accum. Depre. - Store Fixtures & Equip.	146		4830 —	25
26			Accumulated Depreciation-Delivery Equip.	148		900 —	26
27							27
28	i	30	Payroll Taxes Expense	607	1957 —		28
29			Payroll Taxes Payable	226		1957 —	29
30							30
31	j	30	Interest Expense	691	75 —		31
32			Interest Payable	233		75 —	32
33							33
34							34
35							35
36							36
37							37
38							38
39							39
40							40
41							41
42							42
43							43
44							44
45							45

	DATE		DESCRIPTION	POST. REF.	DEBIT	CREDIT	
1	2001		Closing Entries				1
2	June	30	Sales	401	763206 —		2
3			Interest Income	491	1490 —		3
4			Purchases Returns & Allowances	551	919767		4
5			Purchases Discounts	553	434921		5
6			Income Summary	399		77824288	6
7							7
8		30	Income Summary	399	6857116 50		8
9			Sales Returns & Allowances	441		1199452	9
10			Purchases	501		435772 —	10
11			Freight In	506		1602488	11
12			Sales Salaries Expense	601		79760 —	12
13			Office Salaries Expense	602		28980 —	13
14			Stockroom Salaries Expense	603		26220 —	14
15			Payroll Taxes Expense	607		14500 —	15
16			Rent Expense - Garage	611		4200 —	16
17			Utilities Expense	612		9610 —	17
18			Telephone Expense	613		1710 —	18
19			Store Supplies Expense	621		1741 —	19
20			Office Supplies Expense	622		642 —	20
21			Delivery Expense	623		6960 —	21
22			Advertising Expense	624		4060 —	22
23			Rubbish Removal Expense	625		2400 —	23
24			Insurance Expense	631		3145 —	24
25			Loss from Uncollectible Accounts	632		10684 9	25
26			Accounting & Legal Expense	633		4405 —	26
27			Discount Expense on Bank Credit Card Sales	634		24486 1	27
28			Depreciation Expense	641		17730 —	28
29			Interest Expense	691		12345 —	29
30							30
31		30	Income Summary	399	874023 8		31
32			Amy Glenn, Capital	301		874023 8	32
33							33
34		30	Amy Glenn, Capital	301	40800 —		34
35			Amy Glenn, Drawing	302		40800 —	35
36							36
37							37
38							38
39							39
40							40
41							41
42							42
43							43
44							44
45							45

GENERAL JOURNAL

	DATE		DESCRIPTION	POST. REF.	DEBIT	CREDIT	
1	2001		Reversing Entries				1
2	July	1	Interest Income	491	150 —		2
3			Interest Receivable	115		150 —	3
4							4
5		1	Interest Payable	233	75 —		5
6			Interest Expense	691		75 —	6
7							7
8		1	Payroll Taxes Payable	226	1957 —		8
9			Payroll Taxes Expense	607		1957 —	9
10							10
11							11
12							12
13							13
14							14
15							15
16							16
17							17
18							18
19							19
20							20
21							21
22							22
23							23
24							24
25							25
26							26
27							27
28							28
29							29
30							30
31							31
32							32
33							33
34							34
35							35
36							36
37							37
38							38
39							39
40							40
41							41
42							42
43							43
44							44
45							45

GENERAL JOURNAL

PAGE _____

	DATE	DESCRIPTION	POST. REF.	DEBIT	CREDIT	
1						1
2						2
3						3
4						4
5						5
6						6
7						7
8						8
9						9
10						10
11						11
12						12
13						13
14						14
15						15
16						16
17						17
18						18
19						19
20						20
21						21
22						22
23						23
24						24
25						25
26						26
27						27
28						28
29						29
30						30
31						31
32						32
33						33
34						34
35						35
36						36
37						37
38						38
39						39
40						40
41						41
42						42
43						43
44						44
45						45

GENERAL LEDGER

CHART OF ACCOUNTS

Assets
101 Cash
103 Petty Cash Fund
106 Short-Term Investments
111 Accounts Receivable
112 Allowance for Uncollectible Accounts
115 Interest Receivable
121 Merchandise Inventory
131 Prepaid Insurance
133 Store Supplies
135 Office Supplies
141 Land
143 Building
144 Accumulated Depreciation—Building
145 Store Fixtures and Equipment
146 Accumulated Depreciation—Store Fixtures and Equipment
147 Delivery Equipment
148 Accumulated Depreciation—Delivery Equipment

Liabilities
201 Notes Payable
202 Accounts Payable
205 Salaries Payable
221 Social Security Tax Payable
222 Medicare Tax Payable
223 Federal Income Tax Payable
224 State Income Tax Payable
226 Payroll Taxes Payable
231 Sales Tax Payable
233 Interest Payable
251 Mortgage Payable

Owner's Equity
301 Amy Glenn, Capital
302 Amy Glenn, Drawing
399 Income Summary

Revenue
401 Sales
441 Sales Returns and Allowances
491 Interest Income

Costs and Expenses
501 Purchases
506 Freight In
551 Purchases Returns and Allowances
553 Purchases Discount
601 Sales Salaries Expense
602 Office Salaries Expense
603 Stockroom Salaries Expense
607 Payroll Taxes Expense
611 Rent Expense—Garage
612 Utilities Expense
613 Telephone Expense
621 Store Supplies Expense
622 Office Supplies Expense
623 Delivery Expense
624 Advertising Expense
625 Rubbish Removal Expense
631 Insurance Expense
632 Loss From Uncollectible Accounts
633 Accounting and Legal Expense
634 Discount Expense on Bank Credit Card Sales
641 Depreciation Expense
691 Interest Expense

ACCOUNT *Cash* ACCOUNT NO. *101*

DATE		EXPLANATION	POST. REF.	DEBIT	CREDIT	BALANCE DEBIT	BALANCE CREDIT
19X5 June	1	Balance	✓			21 0 8 7 18	
	30		CR36	76 8 0 2 99		97 8 9 0 17	
	30		CP36		92 3 0 1 59	5 5 8 8 58	

ACCOUNT *Petty Cash Fund* ACCOUNT NO. *103*

DATE		EXPLANATION	POST. REF.	DEBIT	CREDIT	BALANCE DEBIT	BALANCE CREDIT
19X5 June	1	Balance	✓			5 0 00	

ACCOUNT *Short-Term Investments* ACCOUNT NO. *106*

DATE		EXPLANATION	POST. REF.	DEBIT	CREDIT	BALANCE DEBIT	BALANCE CREDIT
19X5 June	1	Balance	✓			20 0 0 0 00	
	18		CR36		10 0 0 0 —	10 0 0 0 —	

ACCOUNT *Accounts Receivable* ACCOUNT NO. *111*

DATE		EXPLANATION	POST. REF.	DEBIT	CREDIT	BALANCE DEBIT	BALANCE CREDIT
19X5 June	1	Balance	✓			14 8 2 3 33	
	17		J35		20 —	14 8 0 3 33	
	22		J35		1 1 2 87	14 6 9 0 46	
	26		J35		97 52	14 5 9 2 94	
	30		S35	17 3 6 0 68		31 9 5 3 62	
	30		CR36		16 0 4 4 49	15 9 0 9 13	

ACCOUNT _Allowance for Uncollectible Accounts_   ACCOUNT NO. _112_

DATE		EXPLANATION	POST. REF.	DEBIT	CREDIT	BALANCE DEBIT	BALANCE CREDIT
19X5 June	1	Balance	✓				268 00
	22		J35	112 87			155 13
	30	Adj. Entry	J37		1068 49		1223 62

ACCOUNT _Interest Receivable_   ACCOUNT NO. _115_

DATE		EXPLANATION	POST. REF.	DEBIT	CREDIT	BALANCE DEBIT	BALANCE CREDIT
2001 June	30	Adj. Entry	J37	150 —		150 —	
	30	Reversing Entry	J39		150 —	—	—

ACCOUNT _Merchandise Inventory_   ACCOUNT NO. _121_

DATE		EXPLANATION	POST. REF.	DEBIT	CREDIT	BALANCE DEBIT	BALANCE CREDIT
19X5 June	1	Balance	✓			67862 00	
	30	Adj. Entry	J37		67862 —	—	
	30	Adj. Entry	J37	62738 —		62738 —	

ACCOUNT _Prepaid Insurance_   ACCOUNT NO. _131_

DATE		EXPLANATION	POST. REF.	DEBIT	CREDIT	BALANCE DEBIT	BALANCE CREDIT
19X5 June	1	Balance	✓			4245 00	
	5		CP35	825 —		5070 —	
	10		CR35		100 —	4970 —	
	30	Adj. Entry	J37		3145 —	1825 —	

ACCOUNT *Store Supplies*   ACCOUNT NO. *133*

DATE		EXPLANATION	POST. REF.	DEBIT	CREDIT	BALANCE DEBIT	BALANCE CREDIT
19X5 June	1	Balance	✓			2 2 1 0 00	
	30		CP36	1 1 —		2 2 2 1 —	
	30	Adj. Entry	J37		1 7 4 1 —	4 8 0 —	

ACCOUNT *Office Supplies*   ACCOUNT NO. *135*

DATE		EXPLANATION	POST. REF.	DEBIT	CREDIT	BALANCE DEBIT	BALANCE CREDIT
19X5 June	1	Balance	✓			8 0 0 00	
	30		CP36	1 2 —		8 1 2 —	
	30	Adj. Entry	J37		6 4 2 —	1 7 0 —	

ACCOUNT *Land*   ACCOUNT NO. *141*

DATE		EXPLANATION	POST. REF.	DEBIT	CREDIT	BALANCE DEBIT	BALANCE CREDIT
19X5 June	1	Balance	✓			20 0 0 0 00	

ACCOUNT *Building*   ACCOUNT NO. *143*

DATE		EXPLANATION	POST. REF.	DEBIT	CREDIT	BALANCE DEBIT	BALANCE CREDIT
19X5 June	1	Balance	✓			240 0 0 0 00	

ACCOUNT _Accumulated Depreciation—Building_   ACCOUNT NO. _144_

DATE		EXPLANATION	POST. REF.	DEBIT	CREDIT	BALANCE DEBIT	BALANCE CREDIT
19X5 June	1	Balance	✓				60 0 0 0 00
	30	Adj. Entry	J37		12000 —		72000 —

ACCOUNT _Store Fixtures and Equipment_   ACCOUNT NO. _145_

DATE		EXPLANATION	POST. REF.	DEBIT	CREDIT	BALANCE DEBIT	BALANCE CREDIT
19X5 June	1	Balance	✓			48 0 0 0 00	
	2		CP35	380 —		48380 —	

ACCOUNT _Accum. Deprec.—Store Fixtures and Equip._   ACCOUNT NO. _146_

DATE		EXPLANATION	POST. REF.	DEBIT	CREDIT	BALANCE DEBIT	BALANCE CREDIT
19X5 June	1	Balance	✓				22 0 0 0 00
	30	Adj. Entry	J37		4830 —		26830 —

ACCOUNT _Delivery Equipment_   ACCOUNT NO. _147_

DATE		EXPLANATION	POST. REF.	DEBIT	CREDIT	BALANCE DEBIT	BALANCE CREDIT
19X5 June	1	Balance	✓			9 0 0 0 00	

Name _____ Date _____ Class _____

ACCOUNT *Accumulated Depreciation — Delivery Equipment*   ACCOUNT NO. *148*

DATE		EXPLANATION	POST. REF.	DEBIT	CREDIT	BALANCE DEBIT	BALANCE CREDIT
19X5 June	1	Balance	✓				7 2 0 0 00
	30		J37		9 00 —		8 1 00 —

ACCOUNT *Notes Payable*   ACCOUNT NO. *201*

DATE		EXPLANATION	POST. REF.	DEBIT	CREDIT	BALANCE DEBIT	BALANCE CREDIT
19X5 June	1	Balance	✓				10 0 0 0 00
	29		CP35	5 0 0 0 —			5 0 0 0 —

ACCOUNT *Accounts Payable*   ACCOUNT NO. *202*

DATE		EXPLANATION	POST. REF.	DEBIT	CREDIT	BALANCE DEBIT	BALANCE CREDIT
19X5 June	1	Balance	✓				34 8 9 2 90
	11		J35	5 27 —			34 3 6 5 90
	19		J35	2 50 —			34 1 1 5 90
	30		P35		41 2 66 —		75 3 8 1 90
	30		CP36	56 0 29 40			19 3 5 2 50

ACCOUNT *Salaries Payable*   ACCOUNT NO. *205*

DATE		EXPLANATION	POST. REF.	DEBIT	CREDIT	BALANCE DEBIT	BALANCE CREDIT
2001 June	15		J35		5 9 91 —		5 9 91 00
	15		CP35	5 9 91 —			—
	30		J36		6 0 98 —		6 0 98 —
	30		CP36	6 0 98 —			

ACCOUNT _Social Security Tax Payable_ ACCOUNT NO. _221_

DATE		EXPLANATION	POST. REF.	DEBIT	CREDIT	BALANCE	
						DEBIT	CREDIT
19X5 June	1	Balance	✓				5 5 3 00
	5		CP35	553 —			
	15		J35		570 —		570 —
	19		CP35	570 —			
	30		J36		579 —		579 —

ACCOUNT _Medicare Tax Payable_ ACCOUNT NO. _222_

DATE		EXPLANATION	POST. REF.	DEBIT	CREDIT	BALANCE	
						DEBIT	CREDIT
19X5 June	1	Balance	✓				1 2 7 00
	5		CP35	127 —			
	15		J35		131 —		131 —
	19		CP35	131 —			
	30		J36		133 —		133 —

ACCOUNT _Federal Income Tax Payable_ ACCOUNT NO. _223_

DATE		EXPLANATION	POST. REF.	DEBIT	CREDIT	BALANCE	
						DEBIT	CREDIT
19X5 June	1	Balance	✓				1 7 0 0 00
	5		CP35	1700 —			
	15		J35		1815 —		1815 —
	19		CP35	1815 —			
	30		J36		1833 —		1833 —

ACCOUNT _State Income Tax Payable_ ACCOUNT NO. _224_

DATE		EXPLANATION	POST. REF.	DEBIT	CREDIT	BALANCE	
						DEBIT	CREDIT
19X5 June	1	Balance	✓				5 1 0 00
	12		CP35	510 —			
	15		J35		263 —		263 —
	30		J36		267 —		530 —

ACCOUNT _Payroll Taxes Payable_   ACCOUNT NO. _226_

DATE		EXPLANATION	POST. REF.	DEBIT	CREDIT	BALANCE	
						DEBIT	CREDIT
19X5 June	1	Balance	✓				6 8 0 00
	5		CP35	680 —			
	15		J35		701 —		701 —
	19		CP35	701 —			
	30		J36		712 —		712 —
	30	Adj. Entry	J37		1957 —		2669 —
July	1	Reversing Entry	J39	1957 —			712 —

ACCOUNT _Sales Tax Payable_   ACCOUNT NO. _231_

DATE		EXPLANATION	POST. REF.	DEBIT	CREDIT	BALANCE	
						DEBIT	CREDIT
19X5 June	1	Balance	✓				3 5 7 0 00
	9		CP35	3570 —			
	30		S35		982 68		982 68
	30		CR36		2833 50		3816 18

ACCOUNT _Interest Payable_   ACCOUNT NO. _233_

DATE		EXPLANATION	POST. REF.	DEBIT	CREDIT	BALANCE	
						DEBIT	CREDIT
2001 June	30	Adj. Entry	J37		75 —		75 —
July	1	Reversing Entry	J39	75 —			

ACCOUNT _Mortgage Payable_   ACCOUNT NO. _251_

DATE		EXPLANATION	POST. REF.	DEBIT	CREDIT	BALANCE	
						DEBIT	CREDIT
19X5 June	1	Balance	✓				75 0 0 0 00
	19		CP35	600 —			74400 —

ACCOUNT Amy Glenn, Capital   ACCOUNT NO. 301

DATE		EXPLANATION	POST. REF.	DEBIT	CREDIT	BALANCE DEBIT	BALANCE CREDIT
19X5 June	1	Balance	✓				151 147 03
	30		J38		87402 38		238549 41
	30		J38	40800 —			197749 41

ACCOUNT Amy Glenn, Drawing   ACCOUNT NO. 302

DATE		EXPLANATION	POST. REF.	DEBIT	CREDIT	BALANCE DEBIT	BALANCE CREDIT
19X5 June	1	Balance	✓			37 400 00	
	15		CP35	1700 —		39100 —	
	30		CP36	1700 —		40800 —	
	30	Closing Entry	J38		40800 —		

ACCOUNT Income Summary   ACCOUNT NO. 399

DATE		EXPLANATION	POST. REF.	DEBIT	CREDIT	BALANCE DEBIT	BALANCE CREDIT
2001							
June	30	Adj. Entry	J37	678 62		678 62 —	
	30	Adj. Entry	J37		627 38 —	51 24 —	
	30		J38		77824 288		773 118 88
	30		J38	685716 50			87 402 38
	30	Closing Entry	J38	87402 38			

ACCOUNT Sales   ACCOUNT NO. 401

DATE		EXPLANATION	POST. REF.	DEBIT	CREDIT	BALANCE DEBIT	BALANCE CREDIT
19X5 June	1	Balance	✓				699 603 00
	30		S35		16 378 —		715 981 —
	30		CR36		472 25 —		763 206 —
	30	Closing Entry	J38	763 206 —			

ACCOUNT *Sales Returns and Allowances*   ACCOUNT NO. *441*

DATE		EXPLANATION	POST. REF.	DEBIT	CREDIT	BALANCE DEBIT	BALANCE CREDIT
19X5 June	1	Balance	✓			11 877 00	
	17		J35	20 —		11 897 —	
	26		J35	97 52		11 994 52	
	30	Closing Entry	J38		11 994 52	—	

ACCOUNT *Interest Income*   ACCOUNT NO. *491*

DATE		EXPLANATION	POST. REF.	DEBIT	CREDIT	BALANCE DEBIT	BALANCE CREDIT
19X5 June	1	Balance	✓				740 00
	18		CR36		600 —		1 340 —
	30	Adj. Entry	J37		150 —		1 490 —
	30	Closing Entry	J38	1 490 —			
July	1	Reversing Entry	J39	150 —		150 —	

ACCOUNT *Purchases*   ACCOUNT NO. *501*

DATE		EXPLANATION	POST. REF.	DEBIT	CREDIT	BALANCE DEBIT	BALANCE CREDIT
19X5 June	1	Balance	✓			394 506 00	
	30		P35	41 266 —		435 772 —	
		Closing Entry	J38		435 772 —		

ACCOUNT *Freight In*   ACCOUNT NO. *506*

DATE		EXPLANATION	POST. REF.	DEBIT	CREDIT	BALANCE DEBIT	BALANCE CREDIT
19X5 June	1	Balance	✓			15 654 13	
	8		CP35	192 50		15 846 63	
	18		CP35	178 25		16 024 88	
	30	Closing Entry	J38		16 024 88	—	

ACCOUNT _Purchases Returns and Allowances_   ACCOUNT NO. _551_

DATE		EXPLANATION	POST. REF.	DEBIT	CREDIT	BALANCE DEBIT	BALANCE CREDIT
19X5 June	1	Balance	✓				8 4 2 0 67
	11		J35		527 —		8 9 4 7 67
	19		J35		250 —		9 1 9 7 67
	30	Closing Entry	J38	9 1 9 7 67		—	

ACCOUNT _Purchases Discount_   ACCOUNT NO. _553_

DATE		EXPLANATION	POST. REF.	DEBIT	CREDIT	BALANCE DEBIT	BALANCE CREDIT
19X5 June	1	Balance	✓				4 1 5 8 34
	30		CP36		1 9 0 87		4 3 4 9 21
	30	Closing Entry	J38	4 3 4 9 21		—	

ACCOUNT _Sales Salaries Expense_   ACCOUNT NO. _601_

DATE		EXPLANATION	POST. REF.	DEBIT	CREDIT	BALANCE DEBIT	BALANCE CREDIT
19X5 June	1	Balance	✓			67 5 6 0 00	
	15		J35	6000 —		7 3 5 6 0 —	
	30		J36	6200 —		7 9 7 6 0 —	
	30	Closing Entry	J38		7 9 7 6 0 —	—	

ACCOUNT _Office Salaries Expense_   ACCOUNT NO. _602_

DATE		EXPLANATION	POST. REF.	DEBIT	CREDIT	BALANCE DEBIT	BALANCE CREDIT
19X5 June	1	Balance	✓			25 9 6 0 00	
	15		J35	1540 —		2 7 5 0 0 —	
	30		J36	1480 —		2 8 9 8 0 —	
	30	Closing Entry	J38		2 8 9 8 0 —	—	

102

ACCOUNT *Stockroom Salaries Expense*   ACCOUNT NO. *603*

DATE		EXPLANATION	POST. REF.	DEBIT	CREDIT	BALANCE DEBIT	BALANCE CREDIT
19X5 June	1	Balance	✓			23 7 6 0 00	
	15		J35	1230 —		24990 —	
	30		J36	1230 —		26220 —	
	30	Closing Entry	J38		26220 —		

ACCOUNT *Payroll Taxes Expense*   ACCOUNT NO. *607*

DATE		EXPLANATION	POST. REF.	DEBIT	CREDIT	BALANCE DEBIT	BALANCE CREDIT
19X5 June	1	Balance	✓			11 1 3 0 00	
	15		J35	701 —		11831 —	
	30		J36	712 —		12543 —	
	30	Adj. Entry	J37	1957 —		14500 —	
	30	Closing Entry	J38		14500 —		
July	1	Reversing Entry	J39		1957 —		1957 —

ACCOUNT *Rent Expense—Garage*   ACCOUNT NO. *611*

DATE		EXPLANATION	POST. REF.	DEBIT	CREDIT	BALANCE DEBIT	BALANCE CREDIT
19X5 June	1	Balance	✓			3 8 5 0 00	
	1		CP35	350 —		4200 —	
	30	Closing Entry	J38		4200 —		

ACCOUNT *Utilities Expense*   ACCOUNT NO. *612*

DATE		EXPLANATION	POST. REF.	DEBIT	CREDIT	BALANCE DEBIT	BALANCE CREDIT
19X5 June	1	Balance	✓			9 0 8 5 00	
	1		CP35	525 —		9610 —	
	30	Closing Entry	J38		9610 —		

ACCOUNT _Telephone Expense_   ACCOUNT NO. _613_

DATE		EXPLANATION	POST. REF.	DEBIT	CREDIT	BALANCE DEBIT	BALANCE CREDIT
19X5 June	1	Balance	✓			1 5 0 0 00	
	8		CP35	2 1 0 —		1 7 1 0 —	
	30	Closing Entry	J38		1 7 1 0 —	—	—

ACCOUNT _Store Supplies Expense_   ACCOUNT NO. _621_

DATE		EXPLANATION	POST. REF.	DEBIT	CREDIT	BALANCE DEBIT	BALANCE CREDIT
2001							
June	30	Adj. Entry	J37	1 7 41 —		1 7 41 —	
	30	Closing Entry	J38		1 7 41 —	—	—

ACCOUNT _Office Supplies Expense_   ACCOUNT NO. _622_

DATE		EXPLANATION	POST. REF.	DEBIT	CREDIT	BALANCE DEBIT	BALANCE CREDIT
2001							
June	30	Adj. Entry	J37	6 42 —		6 42 —	
	30	Closing Entry	J38		6 42 —	—	—

ACCOUNT _Delivery Expense_   ACCOUNT NO. _623_

DATE		EXPLANATION	POST. REF.	DEBIT	CREDIT	BALANCE DEBIT	BALANCE CREDIT
19X5 June	1	Balance	✓			6 5 7 0 00	
	10		CP35	2 75 —		6 8 45 —	
	26		CP35	92 —		6 9 37 —	
	30		CP36	23 —		6 9 60 —	
	30	Closing Entry	J38		6 9 60 —	—	—

Name _____ Date _____ Class _____

ACCOUNT *Advertising Expense* ACCOUNT NO. 624

DATE		EXPLANATION	POST. REF.	DEBIT	CREDIT	BALANCE DEBIT	BALANCE CREDIT
19X5 June	1	Balance	✓			3 6 0 0 00	
	3		CP35	460 —		4060 —	
	30	Closing Entry	J38		4060 —	—	—

ACCOUNT *Rubbish Removal Expense* ACCOUNT NO. 625

DATE		EXPLANATION	POST. REF.	DEBIT	CREDIT	BALANCE DEBIT	BALANCE CREDIT
19X5 June	1	Balance	✓			2 2 0 0 00	
	4		CP35	200 —		2400 —	
	30	Closing Entry	J38		2400 —	—	—

ACCOUNT *Insurance Expense* ACCOUNT NO. 631

DATE		EXPLANATION	POST. REF.	DEBIT	CREDIT	BALANCE DEBIT	BALANCE CREDIT
2001 June	30	Adj. Entry	J37	31 45 —		31 45 —	
	30	Closing Entry	J38		31 45 —	—	—

ACCOUNT *Loss from Uncollectible Accounts* ACCOUNT NO. 632

DATE		EXPLANATION	POST. REF.	DEBIT	CREDIT	BALANCE DEBIT	BALANCE CREDIT
2001 June	30	Adj. Entry	J37	1068 49		1068 49	
	30	Closing Entry	J38		1068 49	—	—

ACCOUNT _Accounting and Legal Expense_   ACCOUNT NO. _633_

DATE		EXPLANATION	POST. REF.	DEBIT	CREDIT	BALANCE DEBIT	BALANCE CREDIT
19X5 June	1	Balance	✓			4 2 9 5 00	
	25		CP35	1 1 0 —		4 4 0 5 —	
	30	Closing Entry	J38		4 4 0 5 —	—	—

ACCOUNT _Discount Expense on Bank Credit Card Sales_   ACCOUNT NO. _634_

DATE		EXPLANATION	POST. REF.	DEBIT	CREDIT	BALANCE DEBIT	BALANCE CREDIT
19X5 June	1	Balance	✓			2 2 7 5 30	
	30		CP36	1 7 3 31		2 4 4 8 61	
	30	Closing Entry	J38		2 4 4 8 61	—	—

ACCOUNT _Depreciation Expense_   ACCOUNT NO. _641_

DATE		EXPLANATION	POST. REF.	DEBIT	CREDIT	BALANCE DEBIT	BALANCE CREDIT
2001 June	30	Adj. Entry	J37	1 7 7 30 —		1 7 7 30 —	
	30	Closing Entry	J38		1 7 7 30 —	—	—

ACCOUNT _Interest Expense_   ACCOUNT NO. _691_

DATE		EXPLANATION	POST. REF.	DEBIT	CREDIT	BALANCE DEBIT	BALANCE CREDIT
19X5 June	1	Balance	✓			1 1 2 7 0 00	
	19		CP35	9 60 —		1 2 2 3 0 —	
	29		CP35	4 0 —		1 2 2 7 0 —	
	30	Adj. Entry	J37	7 5 —		1 2 3 4 5 —	
	30	Closing Entry	J38		1 2 3 4 5 —	—	—
July	1	Reversing Entry	J39		7 5 —		7 5 —

ACCOUNTS RECEIVABLE SUBSIDIARY LEDGER

CHARGE ACCOUNT CUSTOMERS

Customer Account Number	Customer Name
1089	Jean Alvarez
2369	Freida Berkley
2745	Max Bukowski
2984	Rose Delaney
3118	James Dolan
4316	Sylvia Gerber
4277	William Hubbard
5081	Kim Lee
5748	Juan Quinones
6281	Miriam Rigroski
6443	Edith Ross
6770	George Sachs
6846	John Schuetz
6907	Stephen Sidorsky
7651	James Tashiko
7649	Carol Thompson
7805	Irene Viola
9623	Abby Washington
9672	Arnold Wexler
9864	Henry Zaccarelli

NAME *Jean Alvarez*   Customer No. _____ 1089

ADDRESS *2682 Hampton Road, Allison Park, PA 15101-2483*

DATE		EXPLANATION	POST. REF.	DEBIT	CREDIT	BALANCE
19X5 June	1	Balance	√			1 2 8 2 82
	2		S35	9 28 56		2 2 1 1 38
	11		CR35		1000 —	1 2 1 1 38

NAME *Freida Berkley*   Customer No. _____ 2369

ADDRESS *7118 Ellsworth Avenue, Pittsburgh, PA 15232-4691*

DATE		EXPLANATION	POST. REF.	DEBIT	CREDIT	BALANCE
19X5 June	1	Balance	√			5 2 16
	19		S35	1 27 20		1 79 36

NAME *Max Bukowski*   Customer No. _____ 2745

ADDRESS *5206 Fifth Avenue, Pittsburgh, PA 15232-8433*

DATE		EXPLANATION	POST. REF.	DEBIT	CREDIT	BALANCE
19X5 June	1	Balance	√			9 86 26
	9		CR35		9 86 26	—
	24		S35	1 53 3 82		1 53 3 82

NAME *Rose Delaney*   Customer No. _____ 2984

ADDRESS *323 Boyce Road, Monroeville, PA 15146-2006*

DATE		EXPLANATION	POST. REF.	DEBIT	CREDIT	BALANCE
19X5 June	1	Balance	√			— 0 —
	3		S35	7 57 90		7 57 90
	25		CR36		7 57 90	—

NAME _James Dolan_ Customer No. _3118_

ADDRESS _523 North Highland Avenue, Pittsburgh, PA 15206-6716_

DATE		EXPLANATION	POST. REF.	DEBIT	CREDIT	BALANCE
19X5 June	1	Balance	✓			1 2 1 47
	5		S35	59 36		1 80 83
	15		S35	1 73 84		3 54 67
	17		J35		20 —	3 34 67
	23		CR36		1 21 47	2 13 20

NAME _Sylvia Gerber_ Customer No. _4316_

ADDRESS _24 Mill Road, Canonsburg, PA 15020-8288_

DATE		EXPLANATION	POST. REF.	DEBIT	CREDIT	BALANCE
19X5 June	1	Balance	✓			2 82 31
	9		S35	59 36		3 41 67
	15		CR35		3 41 67	—
	25		S35	6 09 50		6 09 50

NAME _William Hubbard_ Customer No. _4277_

ADDRESS _6824 South Aiken Avenue, Pittsburgh, PA 15232-2284_

DATE		EXPLANATION	POST. REF.	DEBIT	CREDIT	BALANCE
19X5 June	1	Balance	✓			2 41 6 92
	8		CR35		500 —	1 91 6 92
	20		S35	44 52		1 96 1 44

NAME _Kim Lee_ Customer No. _5081_

ADDRESS _221 Morewood Avenue, Pittsburgh, PA 15213-3308_

DATE		EXPLANATION	POST. REF.	DEBIT	CREDIT	BALANCE
19X5 June	1	Balance	✓			5 10 20
	10		CR35		5 10 20	—
	23		S35	97 52		97 52
	26		J35		97 52	

Name _____ Date _____ Class _____

NAME *Juan Quinones* Customer No. 5748

ADDRESS *18 Beulah Road, Turtle Creek, PA 15145-2339*

DATE		EXPLANATION	POST. REF.	DEBIT	CREDIT	BALANCE
19X5 June	1	Balance	✓			72 93
	22		CR36		72 93	—

NAME *Miriam Rigroski* Customer No. 6281

ADDRESS *4618 Greentree Road, Carnegie, PA 15106-9862*

DATE		EXPLANATION	POST. REF.	DEBIT	CREDIT	BALANCE
19X5 June	1	Balance	✓			– 0 –
	5		S35	424 —		424 —
	18		S35	175 96		599 96

NAME *Edith Ross* Customer No. 6443

ADDRESS *426 Westminister Road, Pittsburgh, PA 15232-7870*

DATE		EXPLANATION	POST. REF.	DEBIT	CREDIT	BALANCE
19X5 June	1	Balance	✓			382 91
	2		CR35		382 91	—
	12		S35	50 88		50 88
	22		S35	2774 02		2824 90

NAME *George Sachs* Customer No. 6770

ADDRESS *1438 Murray Avenue, Pittsburgh, PA 15217-4168*

DATE		EXPLANATION	POST. REF.	DEBIT	CREDIT	BALANCE
19X5 June	1	Balance	✓			– 0 –
	1		S35	116 60		116 60
	8		S35	408 10		524 70
	12		CR35		116 60	408 10

NAME _John Schuetz_   Customer No. _____ 6846

ADDRESS _706 South Avenue, Pittsburgh, PA 15221-7118_

DATE		EXPLANATION	POST. REF.	DEBIT	CREDIT	BALANCE
19X5 June	1	Balance	✓			2 9 1 3 47
	4		CR35		1000 —	1 9 1 3 47
	30		CR36		1000 —	9 1 3 47

NAME _Stephen Sidorsky_   Customer No. _____ 6907

ADDRESS _9321 Eighth Avenue, Homestead, PA 15120-1998_

DATE		EXPLANATION	POST. REF.	DEBIT	CREDIT	BALANCE
19X5 June	1	Balance	✓			7 4 4 12
	8		S35	2 4 3 80		9 8 7 92
	25		CR36		7 4 4 12	2 4 3 80

NAME _James Tashiko_   Customer No. _____ 7651

ADDRESS _828 Braddock Avenue, Pittsburgh, PA 15221-3974_

DATE		EXPLANATION	POST. REF.	DEBIT	CREDIT	BALANCE
19X5 June	1	Balance	✓			1 1 2 87
	22		J35		1 1 2 87	—

NAME _Carol Thompson_   Customer No. _____ 7649

ADDRESS _556 Shady Avenue, Pittsburgh, PA 15217-5944_

DATE		EXPLANATION	POST. REF.	DEBIT	CREDIT	BALANCE
19X5 June	1	Balance	✓			4 2 6 8 02
	8		CR35		4 2 6 8 02	
	17		S35	2 0 2 4 60		2 0 2 4 60

| Name | | Date | | Class | |

NAME *Irene Viola*   Customer No. _____ 7805

ADDRESS *36 St. James Place, Pittsburgh, PA 15232-3519*

DATE		EXPLANATION	POST. REF.	DEBIT	CREDIT	BALANCE
19X5 June	1	Balance	✓			1 9 6 12
	11		S35	6 7 8 40		8 7 4 52
	17		CR35		1 40 70	7 3 3 82
	26		S35	3 9 8 56		1 1 3 2 38

NAME *Abby Washington*   Customer No. _____ 9623

ADDRESS *914 South Negley Avenue, Pittsburgh, PA 15232-2064*

DATE		EXPLANATION	POST. REF.	DEBIT	CREDIT	BALANCE
19X5 June	1	Balance	✓			– 0 –
	13		S35	6 0 4 20		6 0 4 20

NAME *Arnold Wexler*   Customer No. _____ 9672

ADDRESS *57 Brinley Drive, Verona, PA 15147-4753*

DATE		EXPLANATION	POST. REF.	DEBIT	CREDIT	BALANCE
19X5 June	1	Balance	✓			7 6 94
	1		CR35		76 94	———
	11		S35	3 6 2 0 96		3 6 2 0 96
	24		CR36		3 6 2 0 96	———
	30		S35	1 2 2 8 54		1 2 2 8 54

NAME *Henry Zaccarelli*   Customer No. _____ 9864

ADDRESS *793 Amberson Avenue, Pittsburgh, PA 15213-6155*

DATE		EXPLANATION	POST. REF.	DEBIT	CREDIT	BALANCE
19X5 June	1	Balance	✓			4 0 3 81
	3		CR35		4 03 81	———
	23		S35	2 2 0 48		2 2 0 48

ACCOUNTS PAYABLE
SUBSIDIARY LEDGER

CREDITORS

Butler Butcher Block Company
Carnegie Shelving, Inc.
Danish Import Company
Hi-Tech Manufacturing Company
J & K Designs
Nordic Furniture Company
Oxford European Design, Inc.
Woodcraft, Inc.

Name _____ Date _____ Class _____

NAME *Butler Butcher Block Company*   Terms _____ n/30

ADDRESS *1074 Railroad Avenue, Butler, PA 16003-2887* _____

DATE		EXPLANATION	POST. REF.	DEBIT	CREDIT	BALANCE
19X5 June	1	Balance	✓			14 1 2 9 60
	2		P35		12890 —	27 0 1 9 60
	11		CP35	14129 60		12890 —
	16		P35		4984 —	17874 —
	29		CP35	12890 —		4984 —

NAME *Carnegie Shelving Company*   Terms _____ 2/10, n/30

ADDRESS *62 Main Street, Claysville, PA 15323-3029* _____

DATE		EXPLANATION	POST. REF.	DEBIT	CREDIT	BALANCE
19X5 June	1	Balance	✓			1 2 8 1 00
	3		P35		1867 —	3148 —
	5		CP35	1281 —		1867 —
	12		CP35	1867 —		—
	24		P35		1483 —	1483 —

NAME *Danish Import Company*   Terms _____ n/30

ADDRESS *621 Broadway, New York, NY 10026-8243* _____

DATE		EXPLANATION	POST. REF.	DEBIT	CREDIT	BALANCE
19X5 June	1	Balance	✓			5 8 1 4 00
	4		P35		3833 —	9647 —
	16		CP35	5814 —		3833 —
	18		P35		3529 —	7362 —
	22		CP35	3833 —		3529 —

NAME *Hi-Tech Manufacturing Co.*   Terms _____ 1/10, n/30

ADDRESS *1268 Spartan Road, Grand Rapids, MI 49315-5224* _____

DATE		EXPLANATION	POST. REF.	DEBIT	CREDIT	BALANCE
19X5 June	1		✓			3 2 8 5 00
	8		CP35	3285 —		—

NAME _J & K Designs_   Terms _n/60_

ADDRESS _4629 Myers Road, Charlotte, NC 28205-4182_

DATE		EXPLANATION	POST. REF.	DEBIT	CREDIT	BALANCE
19X5 June	1	Balance	✓			4 1 6 8 20
	17		CP35	2000 —		2 1 6 8 20

NAME _Nordic Furniture Company_   Terms _2/10, n/30_

ADDRESS _326 West 27 Street, New York, NY 10051-4921_

DATE		EXPLANATION	POST. REF.	DEBIT	CREDIT	BALANCE
19X5 June	1	Balance	✓			— 0 —
	11		P35		2982 —	2982 —
	17		P35		2021 —	5003 —
	18		CP35	2982 —		2021 —
	19		J35	250 —		1771 —
	22		P35		3924	5695 —
	24		CP35	1771 —		3924 —

NAME _Oxford European Design, Inc._   Terms _n/30_

ADDRESS _246 West 23rd Street, New York, NY 10018-1728_

DATE		EXPLANATION	POST. REF.	DEBIT	CREDIT	BALANCE
19X5 June	1	Balance	✓			5 2 8 6 80
	4		CP35	5 2 8 6 80		
	9		P35		1417 —	1417 —
	11		J35	527 —		890 —
	23		CP35	890 —		
	26		P35		621 —	621 —

NAME _Woodcraft, Inc._   Terms _n/30_

ADDRESS _6291 North Drive, Los Angeles, CA 90038-2934_

DATE		EXPLANATION	POST. REF.	DEBIT	CREDIT	BALANCE
19X5 June	1	Balance	✓			9 2 8 30
	9		P35		1715 —	2643 30

ACCOUNTING STATIONERY

Wood n' Things

Schedule of Accounts Receivable

June 30, 19X5

Jean Alvarez	1	2	11	38
Freida Berkley	1	7	9	36
Max Bukowski	1	5	33	82
James Dolan		2	13	20
Sylvia Gerber		6	09	50
William Hubbard	1	9	61	44
Miriam Rigroski		5	99	96
Edith Ross	2	8	24	90
George Sachs		4	08	10
John Schuetz		9	13	47
Stephen Sidorsky		2	43	80
Carol Thompson	2	0	24	60
Irene Viola	1	1	32	38
Abby Washington		6	04	20
Arnold Wexler	1	2	28	54
Henry Zaccarelli		2	20	48
Total Accounts Receivable	15	9	09	13

Wood n' Things

Schedule of Accounts Payable

June 30, 19X5

Butler-Butcher Block Company		4	98	4 —
Carnegie Shelving Company		1	48	3 —
Danish Import Company		3	52	9 —
J & K Designs		2	16	8 20
Nordic Furniture Company		3	92	4 —
Oxford European Design, Inc.			62	1 —
Woodcraft, Inc.		2	64	3 30
Total Accounts Payable		19	35	2 50

	ACCOUNT NAME	TRIAL BALANCE DEBIT	TRIAL BALANCE CREDIT	ADJUSTMENTS DEBIT	ADJUSTMENTS CREDIT
1	Cash	5588 58			
2	Petty Cash Fund	50 —			
3	Short-Term Investments	10000 —			
4	Accounts Receivable	15909 13			
5	Allowance for Uncollectible Accounts		155 13		c 1068 49
6	Interest Receivable			d 150 —	
7	Merchandise Inventory	67862 —		b 62738 —	a 67862 —
8	Prepaid Insurance	4970 —			e 3145 —
9	Store Supplies	2221 —			f 1741 —
10	Office Supplies	812 —			g 642 —
11	Land	20000 —			
12	Building	240000 —			
13	Accumulated Depreciation—Building		60000 —		h 12000 —
14	Store Fixtures and Equipment	48380 —			
15	Accum. Depre.—Store Fixtures & Equip.		22000 —		h 4830 —
16	Delivery Equipment	9000 —			
17	Accumulated Depreciation—Delivery Equip.		7200 —		h 900 —
18	Notes Payable		5000 —		
19	Accounts Payable		19352 50		
20	Salaries Payable				
21	Social Security Tax Payable		579 —		
22	Medicare Tax Payable		133 —		
23	Federal Income Tax Payable		1833 —		
24	State Income Tax Payable		530 —		
25	Payroll Taxes Payable		712 —		i 1957 —
26	Sales Tax Payable		3816 18		
27	Interest Payable				j 75 —
28	Mortgage Payable		74400 —		
29	Amy Glenn, Capital		151147 03		
30	Amy Glenn, Drawing	40800 —			
31	Income Summary			a 67862 —	b 62738 —
32	Sales		763206 —		
33	Sales Returns & Allowances	11994 52			
34	Interest Income		1340 —		d 150 —
35	Purchases	435772 —			
36	Freight In	16024 88			
37	Purchases Returns & Allowances		9197 67		
38	Purchases Discount		4349 21		
39	Sales Salaries Expense	79760 —			
40	Office Salaries Expense	28980 —			
41	Stockroom Salaries Expense	26220 —			
42	Payroll Taxes Expense	12543 —		i 1957 —	
43	Rent Expense—Garage	4200 —			

Things

sheet

June 30, 19X5

| ADJUSTED TRIAL BALANCE | | INCOME STATEMENT | | BALANCE SHEET | | |
DEBIT	CREDIT	DEBIT	CREDIT	DEBIT	CREDIT	
5588 58				5588 58		1
50 -				50 -		2
10000 -				10000 -		3
15909 13				15909 13		4
	1223 62				1223 62	5
150 -				150 -		6
62738 -				62738 -		7
1825 -				1825 -		8
480 -				480 -		9
170 -				170 -		10
20000 -				20000 -		11
240000 -				240000 -		12
	72000 -				72000 -	13
48380 -				48380 -		14
	26830 -				26830 -	15
9000 -				9000 -		16
	8100 -				8100 -	17
	5000 -				5000 -	18
	19352 50				19352 50	19
						20
	579 -				579 -	21
	133 -				133 -	22
	1833 -				1833 -	23
	530 -				530 -	24
	2669 -				2669 -	25
	3816 18				3816 18	26
	75 -				75 -	27
	74400 -				74400 -	28
	151147 03				151147 03	29
40800 -				40800 -		30
67862 -	62738 -	67862 -	62738 -			31
	763206 -		763206 -			32
11994 52		11994 52				33
	1490 -		1490 -			34
435772 -		435772 -				35
16024 88		16024 88				36
	9197 67		9197 67			37
	4349 21		4349 21			38
79760 -		79760 -				39
28980 -		28980 -				40
26220 -		26220 -				41
14500 -		14500 -				42
4200 -		4200 -				43

	ACCOUNT NAME	TRIAL BALANCE DEBIT	TRIAL BALANCE CREDIT	ADJUSTMENTS DEBIT	ADJUSTMENTS CREDIT
1	Utilities Expense	9610 —			
2	Telephone Expense	1710 —			
3	Store Supplies Expense			f 1741 —	
4	Office Supplies Expense			g 642 —	
5	Delivery Expense	6960 —			
6	Advertising Expense	4060 —			
7	Rubbish Removal Expense	2400 —			
8	Insurance Expense			e 3145 —	
9	Loss from Uncollectible Accounts			c 1068 49	
10	Accounting & Legal Expense	4405 —			
11	Discount Expense on Bank Credit Card Sales	2448 61			
12	Depreciation Expense			h 17730 —	
13	Interest Expense	12270 —		j 75 —	
14		1,124 950 72	1,124 950 72	157 1084 9	157 1084 9
15	Net Income				

Things

sheet (continued)

June 30, 19X5

ADJUSTED TRIAL BALANCE		INCOME STATEMENT		BALANCE SHEET		
DEBIT	CREDIT	DEBIT	CREDIT	DEBIT	CREDIT	
9610 —		9610 —				1
1710 —		1710 —				2
1741 —		1741 —				3
642 —		642 —				4
6960 —		6960 —				5
4060 —		4060 —				6
2400 —		2400 —				7
3145 —		3145 —				8
106849		106849				9
4405 —		4405 —				10
244861		244861				11
17730 —		17730 —				12
12345 —		12345 —				13
1,208 669 21	1,208 669 21	753 578 50	840 980 88	455 090 71	367 688 33	14
		87 402 38			87 402 38	15
		840 980 88	840 980 88	455 090 71	455 090 71	16

Wood n' Things

Income Statement

Year Ended June 30, 19X5

Operating Revenue:					
Sales				$763 206 —	
Less Sales Returns & Allow.				11 994 52	
Net Sales					$751 211 48
Cost of Goods Sold:					
Merchandise Inventory, July 1, 1994				$ 67 862 —	
Purchases		$435 772 —			
Freight In		16 024 88			
Delivered Cost of Purchases		$451 796 88			
Less: Purchases Returns & Allow.	$ 9 197 67				
Purchases Discounts	4 349 21	13 546 88			
Net Delivered Cost of Purchases			438 250 —		
Total Merchandise Available for Sale			$506 112 —		
Less Merchandise Inventory, June 30, 1995			62 738 —		
Cost of Goods Sold				443 374 —	
Gross Profit on Sales				$307 837 48	
Operating Expenses:					
Sales Salaries Expense			$ 79 760 —		
Office Salaries Expense			28 980 —		
Stockroom Salaries Expense			26 220 —		
Payroll Taxes Expense			14 500 —		
Rent Expense – Garage			4 200 —		
Utilities Expense			9 610 —		
Telephone Expense			1 710 —		
Store Supplies Expense			1 741 —		
Office Supplies Expense			642 —		
Delivery Expense			6 960 —		
Advertising Expense			4 060 —		
Rubbish Removal Expense			2 400 —		
Insurance Expense			3 145 —		
Loss from Uncollectible Accounts			1 068 49		
Accounting & Legal Expense			4 405 —		
Discount Expense on Bank Credit Card Sales			2 448 61		
Depreciation Expense			17 730 —		
Total Operating Expenses				209 580 10	
Net Income from Operations				$ 98 257 38	
Other Income					
Interest Income			$ 1 490 —		
Other Expenses					
Interest Expense			12 345 —		
Net Nonoperating Expense				10 855 —	
Net Income for Year				$ 87 402 38	

Amy Glenn, Capital, July 1, 1994			$151 147 03
Net Income for Year	$8 740 2 38		
Less Withdrawals for Year	40 800 —		
Increase in Capital			46 602 38
Amy Glenn, Capital, June 30, 1995			$197 749 41

Wood n' Things

Balance Sheet

June 30, 19X5

Assets					
Current Assets					
Cash			$ 5 588 58		
Petty Cash Fund			50 —		
Short-Term Investments			10 000 —		
Accounts Receivable	$ 15 909 13				
Less Allowance for Uncollectible Accounts	1 223 62		14 685 51		
Interest Receivable			150 —		
Merchandise Inventory			62 738 —		
Prepaid Expenses					
Prepaid Insurance	$ 1 825 —				
Store Supplies	480 —				
Office Supplies	170 —		2 475 —		
Total Current Assets				$95 687 09	
Plant and Equipment					
Land			$ 20 000 —		
Building	$ 240 000 —				
Less Accumulated Depreciation	72 000 —		168 000 —		
Store Fixtures & Equipment	$ 48 380 —				
Less Accumulated Depreciation	26 830 —		21 550 —		
Delivery Equipment	$ 9 000 —				
Less Accumulated Depreciation	8 100 —		900 —		
Total Plant & Equipment				210 450 —	
Total Assets				306 137 09	
Liabilities & Owner's Equity					
Current Liabilities					
Notes Payable			$ 5 000 —		
Accounts Payable			19 352 50		
Social Security Tax Payable			579 —		
Medicare Tax Payable			133 —		
Federal Income Tax Payable			1 833 —		
State Income Tax Payable			530 —		
Payroll Taxes Payable			2 669 —		
Sales Tax Payable			3 816 18		
Interest Payable			75 —		
Total Current Liabilities				$33 987 68	
Long-Term Liabilities					
Mortgage Payable				74 400 —	
Total Liabilities				$108 387 68	
Owner's Equity					
Amy Glehn, Capital				197 749 41	
Total Liabilities & Owner's Equity				$306 137 09	

	Debit	Credit
Cash	5 5 8 8 58	
Petty Cash Fund	50 —	
Short-Term Investments	1 0 0 0 0 —	
Accounts Receivable	1 5 9 0 9 13	
Allowance for Uncollectible Accounts		1 2 2 3 62
Interest Receivable	1 50 —	
Merchandise Inventory	6 2 7 3 8 —	
Prepaid Insurance	1 8 2 5 —	
Store Supplies	4 80 —	
Office Supplies	1 70 —	
Land	2 0 0 0 0 —	
Building	2 4 0 0 0 0 —	
Accumulated Depreciation - Building		7 2 0 0 0 —
Store Fixtures & Equipment	4 8 3 8 0 —	
Accumulated Depreciation - Store Fixtures & Equipment		2 6 8 3 0 —
Delivery Equipment	9 0 0 0 —	
Accumulated Depreciation - Delivery Equipment		8 1 0 0 —
Notes Payable		5 0 0 0 —
Accounts Payable		1 9 3 5 2 50
Social Security Tax Payable		5 79 —
Medicare Tax Payable		1 33 —
Federal Income Tax Payable		1 8 3 3 —
State Income Tax Payable		5 30 —
Payroll Taxes Payable		2 6 9 —
Sales Tax Payable		3 8 1 6 18
Interest Payable		75 —
Mortgage Payable		7 4 4 0 0 —
Amy Glenn, Capital		1 9 7 7 4 9 41
	4 1 4 2 9 0 71	4 1 4 2 9 0 71

MANAGERIAL ANALYSIS QUESTIONS

MANAGERIAL ANALYSIS QUESTIONS

1. Accountants often compare a firm's current assets to its current liabilities in order to assess the ability of the firm to pay its short-term debt. A current ratio (current assets divided by current liabilities) of 2 to 1 or better is usually considered safe. Compute the current ratio of Wood n' Things for the years 19X4 and 19X5. (Refer to the balance sheet on pages 16 and 17 for the 19X4 data.) Comment on the trend in this ratio at Wood n' Things. Has the firm's ability to pay its current liabilities as they become due improved or worsened?

2. There is no provision for income tax shown on the income statement of Wood n' Things. Why?

3. What is the advantage to Wood n' Things of having a separate Purchases Returns and Allowances account rather than crediting returns and allowances to the Purchases account directly?

4. It is a policy of Wood n' Things to deposit all cash receipts intact in the bank each day. What are the benefits to Wood n' Things of such a policy?

5. Wood n' Things is currently considering the idea of eliminating its charge accounts and accepting only bank credit cards if a customer wants to buy on credit. What are the advantages of accepting only bank credit cards? The disadvantages?

6. Accountants often compare the cost of goods sold and the gross profit on sales to net sales when analyzing the income statement. Compute the cost of goods sold percentage (cost of goods sold divided by net sales) and the gross profit percentage (gross profit on sales divided by net sales) for the years 19X4 and 19X5. (Refer to the income statement on pages 15 and 16 for the 19X4 data.) What is the significance of these percentages in analyzing the ability of Wood n' Things to control costs and improve net income?

7. The inventory turnover represents the time period it takes from the purchase of inventory until its sale. Inventory turnover is calculated by dividing the cost of goods sold by the average inventory. Compute the inventory turnover for Wood n' Things for 19X4 and 19X5. (Refer to the income statement on pages 15 and 16 for the 19X4 data.) Comment on the trend in this ratio at Wood n' Things.

8. Wood n' Things has a policy of placing excess cash in short-term investments such as certificates of deposit and U.S. Treasury notes. What is an advantage of this policy? What care must be taken in carrying out such a policy?

9. During 19X5, what was the total cost to Wood n' Things of the employees on its payroll?

10. What are the advantages of Wood n' Things having an outside payroll service company prepare its payroll records, checks, and tax returns? What are the disadvantages?